BECAUSE YOU NEVER ASKED

BECAUSE YOU NEVER ASKED

A collection of essays by Post Consumer Man (Jerome Grapel)

BOOK ONE

The New Atlantian Library

The New Atlantian Library
is an imprint of
ABSOLUTELY AMAZING eBOOKS

Published by Whiz Bang LLC, 926 Truman Avenue, Key West, Florida 33040, USA

For information contact:
Publisher@AbsolutelyAmazingEbooks.com

ISBN-13: 978-0615996356
ISBN-10: 0615996353

This book is dedicated to my mother Ann.
She waited almost a century for this.

BECAUSE YOU NEVER ASKED

Note to the Reader: Many of these essays contain cross-references to other essays. Being that this collection is a small part of the writer's output, many of the essays referenced do not appear in this book, something that should not effect their effectiveness.

INTRODUCTION

I began writing essays in the early 90's, the collection "Because You Never Asked" being a fractional but representative cross-section of an output that is still in progress today. I restrict their content to anything that may be relevant since the dawn of time to the end of eternity. They've given me a kind of therapeutical way to voice my objections to the paradigm of our culture and the negativity it is leading us into. All cultures attempt to inculcate their constituents into someone's narrow minded, self-serving version of reality and this book is an attempt to translate these subterfuges into the truth. Although a number of my earliest essays are included in this collection, the vast majority of them are more contemporary. Regardless of their chronology, they should all still be pertinent to whatever is happening at this moment.

- Jerome Grapel
A/K/A Post Consumer Man

PART I

THE BASIC POST CONSUMER MAN: CHALLENGING THE MOST ACCEPTED ASSUMPTIONS OF OUR WAY OF LIFE

TECHNOLOGY

(This essay was written around the early 1990's, before the inception of the online lifestyle)

I've always been fond of travel. I don't see how anyone setting forth the philosophical pretensions I am in these pages could make claim to such wisdom without having seen a variety of cultures and places. If one of the attributes of a good philosopher is to have gotten about a bit, at least I qualify on that account.

I recently went to my local travel agent to secure passage away from the usual tedium of my every day existence. Today's travel agency bears little resemblance to the one of just ten years ago. It now more resembles some kind of strategic air command bunker swimming in the electronic wizardry we generally associate with underground war rooms and nuclear attacks. It seems that such pulsating gadgetry is now essential if one is to fly from point A to point B.

I'm not convinced of this.

Going to the travel agent is never a routine experience for me. I've finally begun to understand why this is so: these enclaves of technological ostentation are only set to work smoothly if you are going to Disneyland or Las Vegas. What's more, you must be going for such respectably measured time frames as a weekend, a week, or 14 days and 13 nights. If you are one of the masses that form this travel minion, it is amazing what kind of bang you will get for your buck: they'll throw in a car, various complimentary steaks and baked potatoes, a trip to Snake World, a floor show full of girls dressed only in a piece of string, etc. etc. (drinks not included).

If you are one of the subversive characters that fall outside these parameters, your airline ticket will cost about the same as the down payment on a house. You will then have to change planes in Orlando, Atlanta, New York, London, Frankfurt and who knows what other global economy air hub, before finally arriving to your destination in a blood shot daze at one in the morning. Unfortunately, the one piece of luggage you had the guts to check is spinning patiently on a carousel in Las Vegas.

Predictably, I fall into the latter category and the high tech, war room scenario has done little to lessen my burden.

My recent trip to the travel agent was typical. It all started innocently enough with a smiling young girl asking how she could help me. As I sketched my itinerary, the smile began to fade and the barest hint of a furl began insinuating itself into her forehead. With a noticeable lack of aplomb, she turned to her green-faced computer and settled into a frenzied attack on the keyboard worthy of anything I'd ever seen from Liberace. As she feverishly pecked away, I could not help noticing the rest of the office, which danced to a rhythm of machines hissing, belching, flashing and clacking away on all sides. Unattended organisms of metal and plastic were spitting out fully completed tickets to, undoubtedly, Las Vegas and

Disneyland. I could only sit and marvel as I awaited my fate.

Eventually, after what seemed to be an interminable interlude of grunts, sighs, and other ambiguous sounds and punctuations not befitting the respectable girl attending me, an unintelligible string of letters resembling a series of Polish surnames without enough vowels, began flashing on the screen. Much to my amazement, the young girl knew exactly what it meant; it meant I was screwed and we had to start again.

At this point I must defend myself. Although my itinerary was not the "Wally World" one so comfortably serviced by our travel industry, I was not going to anywhere so remote as the dark side of the moon or Youngstown, Ohio. I am not on any National Geographic assignment in search of the almost extinct Panda-Koala, last seen in the shrouded mists of the Himalayan headwaters of the Yangtze River. I was simply trying to get to a well-known island in the Mediterranean Sea.

To make a long story even longer, I spent the next hour sitting patiently, examining brochures for Club Med, golf getaways, Busch Gardens, Mardi Gras, tennis camps, and other such respectable destinations where they really want you to go, while the unfortunate young lady working on my case tried to crack it. As the lunch hour approached, I could feel the tension rising. Phone calls were made, the boss was consulted, and the athletic rhapsody on the computer keyboard continued. There were even moments of delirious expectation – at one point we thought we had it at a remarkably low price, but the bubble burst when we found the deal only applied on a Leap Year for those of

Cherokee descent. It was finally decided, by mutual consent, that I'd return in two days, when the verdict would be rendered.

It's moments like this when I begin to feel, down to the deepest pith of my consciousness, the insanity of our occidental life style. This feeling is not confined to travel agents. Each year I regularly attend a big time professional tennis tournament held near my home. Tennis scoreboards used to be manually operated, a perfectly reasonable method considering the pace at which tennis scores change. Now all the scoreboards are computerized extravaganzas that break down or malfunction with dependable punctuality. This lunacy extends to banks, supermarkets, ticket agencies and a whole host of places where the 21st century has already arrived. Sometimes I have to blink or pinch myself ... then I have to ask if I'm getting in and out of these places with more facility than in the "old days."

I'm not against technology. But there is a fine line between using it rationally to secure our well-being and using it recklessly in a way that becomes destructive. Our technological accomplishments are running way ahead of our ability to improve ourselves emotionally. This is a dangerous combination.

The problem with technology is that its development and utilization are under the almost complete dominion of the "Business Tyranny" (see essay "The Revolution and Capitalism"). The motor that drives it all is the incentive to make money. It's not unreasonable to say that this arrangement has spurred on the spectacular success we've had in this area, but it is time to step back and reassess.

This incentive to develop technology based purely on doing business is becoming very destructive. We are burning noxious fuels in unnecessary quantities, we are creating unhealthy amounts of waste, we are destroying important animal habitat, we are clearing forests and jungles that provide ecological functions, just as the filled in marshes and swamps do. If we cannot find a way to advance our technologies without resorting purely to the degrading incentive to make money, then I'm afraid we will not reach any higher evolutionary realization as a species. We have made this incentive to make money the focal point, the centerpiece, the foundation of our system of values. It is beginning to have a corrosive effect on our personalities. If the amounts of anti-social behavior our society now spawns are bordering on the unacceptable, it's not because we've moved away from some simple minded concept of God, or that our families are breaking apart, or that our kids are seeing too many hairy genitals, or some other flat headed, Bill Bennett kind of chicken soup pseudo-wisdom. No!

It's because we have given ourselves over, almost exclusively, to "doing business."

If we cannot eventually transcend this way of motivating ourselves and find a more altruistic, rational road to technological development, it will end up consuming us.

And the Great Pyramids will lie in ruins once again.

Relevant material: *"Julio Senador warned us at the beginning of this century (meaning the 20th century), referring himself to Castilla, that each tree sacrificed was another step towards misery and tyranny." From the book, "Un Mundo que Agoniza" (A World in Agony), by the Spaniard, Miguel Delibes.*

"You will remember that one or two wise men amongst our ancestors (wise men truly, although not in the estimation of the world) dared to doubt the propriety of the word "progress" applied to the advancement of our civilization (... and believed in) principles that would have taught our species to submit itself to the natural laws instead of trying to intervene." From the short story "Discussion Between Monos and Una," by the tortured genius, Edgar Allen Poe.

"No fighting in the War Room!" uttered by the President of the United States (Peter Sellers) in the great movie, Dr. Strangelove.

POST CONSUMER MAN

Why is it that I philosophically go to war using the name "Post Consumer Man"?

If I am going to sit here and bitch and complain about this or that over the course of a decade, piling up a mountain of paper that has now ascended close to the 600-page mark, it is essential to be constantly honing and shaping the intellectual clay of the message. Some recent revelations with regard to the positions staked out by my most habitual ideological foes – people on the "right," market devotees, conservatives, etc. – have encouraged me to further define the essence of Post Consumer Man.

For this writer, the original root of all maladies that might be badgering our existence is an unconscious tendency to consume that is being forced upon us by the economic concept we are currently living under. If we could find some way to temper this destructive, adolescent consumptive compulsion, which is being artificially driven in the name of economic "success," many of the problems stubbornly assailing our species (and all the other species) would begin to heal like a disappearing rash. Surprisingly enough, Post Consumer Man is not a dogmatic ideologue. He can accept an infinite variety of public-private sector combinations, of market driven or regulated business activity, of government interference or indifference. All he asks is that the system, whatever it might be, does not demand consumption. It should be a system that allows the citizens to go about their business in a more natural way, in a way that more reflects what they might really need and not what they are convinced (bludgeoned?, brain washed?) to need.

Unlike the artist Paul Gauguin, naively fleeing to the South Seas in an attempt to find that pure, natural, "Paradise Found" state of existence, Post Consumer Man is not looking back. Post Consumer Man is looking forward. Post Consumer Man accepts the benefits of technology, but would like to see it used for more rational purposes. Post Consumer Man wants to live comfortably. Post Consumer Man is not asking you to sacrifice anything. He is simply asking you to look at your life in a different way, to reassess what is important to you.

Post Consumer Man is a new kind of human being, a person who, without really changing his or her comfort level (in the end, it would most likely enhance such) has decided to need less. But he really hasn't decided anything. It should happen naturally, triggered by a system that does not constantly seduce him into consuming. It would be a system that can find a way to assimilate a drop in sales and production without causing distress to the work force. It would be an economic system – or, in other words, a way to develop and distribute the world's resources – that could at least give us a choice to consume less if the good sense in such became apparent.

This essay started to take form when I began to realize that all the people from the "right" who I habitually fence with intellectually – and we are talking about <u>all</u>, 100%, no exceptions – always threw me the same carrot when agreeing with me on something. "One thing I do agree with you on Jerry, yes, you have a point there, it is excessive, I'm not an extravagant person myself, but yes, it's become abusive, we can't go on like this forever, no, no, this consumption thing Jerry, I myself do not consume ...." etc., etc. Without exception – although one claiming to have one's consumption habits under control is probably fibbing in the same way a man boasts of his feminine conquests – all my "free market cowboy" friends, at the very least, pay lip service to the idea that we should consume less.

And now they've fallen into a philosophical trap. There is a contradiction here that can't be resolved if they are going to continue being fundamentalist zealots adhering strictly to the Bible of current neo-liberal, free market dogma. They kneel before the altar of a system that cannot accommodate even small amounts of sales-production slow down, let alone a true change in cultural philosophy.

I have an old friend from high school who eloquently defends conservative economic rhetoric. He likes to say that in a free society like ours, with free markets and individual liberties and the whole bag of groceries, people have the choice not to consume. In a superficial way, he is correct. But from a practical point of view, under the rules of the road he adheres to, it is almost an inexistent option. It's something like saying you have the choice to not take your hand out of the fire.

It's true, a person could be born into a culture where he or she, almost from the beginning of their self awareness, is bombarded with thousands of commercial images, day after day, morning, noon and night, thousands of attempts to sell you something every week, hundreds of thousands, nay, millions of such persuasive images over the course of a lifetime, and, in spite of all that, buy hardly anything. It is not only possible, it happens. People win millions in the lottery too.

But let's put aside the abstract endeavors at persuasive manipulation and look at the merciless reality of life in the real world, where less consumption becomes no option at all. A person like myself, Post Consumer Man, who lives comfortably – well fed, clothed, housed, using the modern accouterments of electricity, indoor plumbing, a reasonable array of cooking devices and transport possibilities, etc., – is probably spending a microscopic percentage of what the average Monday Night Football Yokel is spending to fulfill his criteria for that vague notion known as happiness. This makes Post Consumer Man a far more dangerous threat to the neo-liberal marketeers than Osama Bin Laden could ever be. It is a way of perceiving things that would take them down quicker than a collapsing Twin Tower.

Unfortunately, as things stand now, it would also cause a tremendous amount of upheaval and hardship. People would be out of work, with no means to sustain themselves, etc., etc. Every time the Gross National Product (and it is gross) or the rate of economic growth falls just a few percentage points, the system and the lives of millions are thrown into a crisis mode. Imagine if the Post Consumer Man style of life became a trend and that hardhearted concept we call "economic growth" fell 10, 20, 40%! That would not be a crisis. It would be a nuclear holocaust.

No, less consumption, under the current rules, is not an option.

Let's get a bit more schematic in trying to further illuminate these concepts: Let's say we have a community of about 500 people who have lived self sufficiently for generations, growing their food and using the materials available to them to exist comfortably (something like an Amish thing). Everyone participates in the work; everyone shares in the bounty. And then, one day, someone gets the bright idea to build a trough connecting the river with their farmland so they can more easily water it. The work is done and it works to perfection. They can now do the same work with 100 less people. What will they do? Draw lots to see who can stay and who has to go? Of course not. They will delegate the work in a different manner. Maybe they'll spruce up the baseball field, or learn how to play the trombone, or write poetry, or even produce something new with the extra time they have. The important thing is that they don't have to consume more in order to keep people working and sustained in their needs.

If this were an enterprise in the global economy of today, this option is not there. Your business must always be looking to cut costs, both for increased earnings and competitiveness. It's pure hardball. No romantic notions allowed. It's the jungle. Everyone is a predator and everyone is prey. Those 100 people from our self-sufficient community are now out on the street. (In the real world, their project would probably have been "privatized"). Perhaps the system (economy) is dynamic enough to absorb them somewhere else. Perhaps not. But under no circumstance are they allowed not to produce. In order for them to sustain themselves, the consumption cannot stop.

My conservative high school buddy recently asked me a good question. "Would you have the government impose rules on consumption, tell us what we can and can't buy, etc.?"

Post Consumer Man does not want the government telling people what they can have or not have, anymore than you the reader does. Ironically, if we continue on the course my conservative friends advocate, that's exactly what could happen. What Post Consumer Man envisions is a system that naturally moves us away from consumption, just as the one we have naturally leads us to consume. In the past, all changes in the economic system were usually driven by a yearning for justice, for a more equitable distribution of the Earth's riches. It might be said that the current system has already served much of its purpose in that it has both created and distributed a good amount of wealth. Although there is still much to do in this sense – especially with regard to third world inclusion, where the exploitation rather than the inclusion of such seems to be a fundamental aspect of the current system's survival – the problem is no longer the ability to provide for all, but the more rational use of our technology in doing so. If we could create that system that moves us away from the current frivolous consumption, the rest would fall into place.

How to do it? Post Consumer Man has a few ideas floating around in his head, rough drafts, experimental concepts, notions to be considered, debated, honed, worked upon, looked into and forever evolved as time goes on. No sacred dogma, unimpeachable correctness or unquestioned line of thought. Everything is always subject to doubt, even, for instance, private energy companies or commercial media conglomerates.

Post Consumer Man believes that the "global economy" is good in that it is global. "Globality," in a world that is more and more connected, is a laudable goal that should be strived for. But what we now call the global economy serves selfish interests in search of dubious goals (over consumption leading to a litany of undesired results). In place of a private sector global economy, I might suggest a global economy of well integrated, well coordinated public sector services that would provide the basics of a modern life style and a foundation of employment for those who might need it. Such things as energy and water supply, health care, waste removal, a blueprint of basic transport services, communications devices, infrastructure maintenance and development, public recreation facilities, etc., could be administered in a kind of federal global system.

The way in which electronic media functions – primarily TV – must be overhauled as well. It should no longer be a forum that is directly linked to commercial interests. We must find a way for it to operate that allows it a certain degree of independence from both governmental and commercial pressures.

Contrary to what you might now think, Post Consumer Man envisions a thriving private sector as well, but not one dominated by the impersonal omnipotence of powerful corporate giants. He sees a far-flung galaxy of local small businesses in direct contact with their customers, businesses that survive on their merits without the use of massive marketing devices like TV.

Certainly, none of these ideas are currently in favor, but they have been discredited by self-interests out to maintain their predominance. I ask the reader not to discard any ideas without objectively considering them, perhaps a utopian thought given the mind pollution we've all been force fed for so long.

The important thing is to define the goal. If the goal is to move us away from irrational consumption, the system can be found to do it. The more difficult task is the emotional one – a world full of Post Consumer Men and Women who understand that the next step forward is to have less materially so we can have more emotionally.

A BUSINESS OPPORTUNITY

(2/06. Obviously, this essay was written before "The Fall of Tiger Woods." I'll have more to say about that later on.)

One of the more magnetic personalities in the world these days is the undeniably best golfer in the world, Tiger Woods (for more, see essay "Tiger Robinson"). It is not often that an athlete of such extraordinary talent is coupled with a positive kind of charisma that translates into a bullet proof marketing infallibility. Talent, sex appeal, style, a droolable Swedish wife ... Tiger is the whole package and more. With the help of his own good instincts and intelligence, he has been sold and packaged with a shrewdness bordering on perfection. Not being one to believe in anyone's image, I would take a certain degree of comfort if he were found one night in a cheap motel with a bag of blow and a crack whore.

That would truly be the end of the empire.

In any event, late one Sunday afternoon, I was potatoed up on the couch doing the zapper thing, when I caught a glimpse of Tiger strolling down a fairway. The beautiful off red color of his perfectly fitting shirt seemed Byronesque against the manicured emerald background of the golf course. I put the zapper down and decided to stay for awhile. I am not a golfer. This is a perfect example of Tiger Power at work.

So there he was, His Majesty, in all the glory of his mature vigor, fending off a host of dragons on his way to a playoff victory (was there ever a doubt?). When the banal creature opposing him sealed his doom with the decisive miss, I adjourned to the shower to purge my body of the day's accumulated inclemency. In a wasteful display of American irresponsibility, I left the TV on as I succumbed to the hygienic call.

When I returned, one of America's great television traditions, "60 Minutes," was trying to make some money for CBS. I've already devoted some unflattering remarks to this program (see essay, "Animal Rights and 60 Minutes"), but my Sunday evening inertia was such that I plopped myself down and robotically began to watch.

The segment in question had to do with a biotech company from California that had perfected a drug or serum that would combat radiation sickness. This could be very useful if one of our nation's seemingly infinite amount of enemies ever managed the dirty deed of a nuclear incursion.

It didn't take long for my mind to begin drifting away from all this. Fear has become the currency of American governance. Try as they might, I am still not afraid, maybe because a nuclear attack would be our just desserts for the lunacy rampant in our cultural dementia; for the dirty games we play. "You reap what you sow." Shouldn't all the religious fanatics on every side of every conflict know this? It's really not that complicated.

And then ... an executive of the radiation serum company said something that blew me away (ha, ha).

" ... and we began to realize that if there were a nuclear attack on one of our major cities, there would be a tremendous market for our product."

I immediately burst out laughing. It was as if I were watching a satirical version of the news – you know, Jon Stewart or Stephen Colbert – and the comedian had hit on a great line. But this was "60 Minutes," America's one hour of sobriety, of straight talking, no nonsense journalism meant to educate and prepare us to be the informed citizens a healthy democracy demands, badda-boom, yadda, yadda.

The first image that came to my mind was from the comic strip "Yosemite Sam." One of its habitual characters, the undertaker, uses the business slogan, "you plug 'em, we plant 'em." I laughed again at my own geniality and returned my attention to the TV. I fully expected the Rolex-wristed businessman to be a bit embarrassed or contrite for such an insensitive remark. "Well ... you know, I don't mean it like that ... if such an unfortunate thing ever ..." (Cue Steve Martin) But noooo! He just went on with his blather as if nothing could be more normal, as if he were talking about a possible windfall market for widgets or dry wall.

I then expected the CBS commentator to step in and be contrite for him. "You mean ... and let's hope we never have to face such a ..." But noooo! We are talking about the market here, no joke, what could be more serious?

Adding to the tragic-comic aspects of all this is the fact that you don't have to be a nuclear-bio-serum-salesman to understand ... Eureka! ... that a nuclear attack will create a market not only for <u>your</u> product, but a virtual plethora of products. How about morgues, or ambulances, or firefighting equipment, or waste removal, or bandages, crutches and wheel chairs, or Geiger counters, or, or ... my God, one good nuclear attack could probably save the economy. I think Detroit would be perfect. What the hoo have they done in Detroit lately to help the economy? Let's wipe 'em clean and encourage economic growth with the nuclear clean up sector, an industry we still lead the world in.

I began to roll some boardroom scenarios around in my mind: An aide bursts into the room and happily proclaims, "Great news! Osama just went on TV again. He's threatened to wipe out the whole east coast with a dirty bomb." Joy, jubilation, the company's stock triples in one day (and guess what? Dick Cheney owns a ton of it).

Or how about: An aide bursts into the room, a look of distress on his face. "The Israelis and Palestinians have just made peace! Hamas and Hezbollah vow to fight terrorism. We're ruined!" (Cheney sold his stock the day before)

But seriously folks, the incident that spawned this essay can now be seen as a microcosm for America's whole economic scheme. This country has invested more heavily in enemies than in any other thing. Enemies have become the foundation of our economy's well being. Enemies provide employment. Enemies provide profits. If you don't get it by now, just ask Halliburton (Cheney's brother-in-law holds chunks of stock.)

Enemies provide us with an identity. What would America be without enemies?

PLANNED OBSOLESCENCE

(11/06)

"Planned obsolescence" is a concept inherent in the type of economic system currently tyrannizing the world, and any person with an intellectual curiosity beyond Ohio State-Michigan has some consciousness of this. In the essay "The Cell Phone," I got off a good rant on the subject, but a recent happening in my life has intensified my feelings. Honestly folks, the extent to which this idea is now practiced goes beyond stupidity and into the realm of <u>immorality</u>. (For you religious people, the proper word is "sinful").

For the last two and a half years or so, the anti-reality that enters my home through a TV screen has been provided by a nice little 14" color TV by Toshiba. It was given to me, amongst other things, by the Nielsen Ratings people, who had randomly picked me to be one of their subjects. They offered a much bigger one that I refused, such smaller size being more in harmony with the dimensions of the room. I mention this because it means I haven't bought a TV for almost 10 years, a fact that becomes relevant later on. In any event, the little Toshiba works perfectly – except for one thing.

About two weeks ago, I couldn't get the remote to work. I replaced the batteries, bought a new "universal" remote, went back to the electronics store to see if I was setting it up properly, replaced it with a better one – all to no avail.

When the smoke had cleared, it seemed the TV itself was at fault – probably. I say "probably" because there has never been a definitive prognosis on the matter. While navigating my way through the vast galaxy known as the electronics industry, I began to realize it was a problem too minute for anyone to deal with. After explaining my travails and woes, the salesperson would say something like, "yeah, it could be the TV, sometimes the sensors stop working," and then turn to someone who was looking to buy a razor thin, wrap around Plasma-HD-VCR-DVD-DSL-Mega-Comcast-Digital-Super Galactic-Internet-IPod-Home-Entertainment extravaganza.

I felt like a guy wearing a leather helmet in a football game.

The best I could get was a halfhearted suggestion to check with an electronics repair shop on so-and-so street. Surprisingly, it was only two blocks from my house and I had never noticed it. Rumor had it they repaired TV's there.

Being that I could walk to it, I decided to check it out. Sure enough, there it was, on my neighborhood's main commercial street, wedged in between a perfectly groomed real estate office oozing prosperity and a trendy art gallery. The inside of the place was hiding behind the defenses of those tinted windows where one can see out but not in. Etched on the glass was the name "ELECTRONIC CONNECTION" with the word "REPAIRS" under it, and then the words "TV's," VCR's" and a few others that have faded from memory. A wooden door peeling white paint flanked the tinted glass panel. It seemed to be the entrance.

Could this be the last TV repair shop in the world?

I felt like a character in an Alfred Hitchcock movie when I finally decided to try the door. The anxiety increased as it surprisingly gave way to the light pressure of my hand. Miracle! The store was open. There was no tinkle of bells as I stepped through the threshold into a cave-like environment whose only light filtered eerily in through the tinted glass. The place was unexpectedly clean and uncluttered, but had an otherworldly quality, as if one had just entered another dimension (cue the Twilight Zone music). A doorway without a door suggested the presence of another room, filled with electronic paraphernalia in various states of repair and disrepair. Behind a steel grey desk to my right sat a non-descript middle-aged man. Chances are, this was the "repairman." He seemed vaguely aware of my presence as he stared at a technical magazine (this was encouraging). The whole scene was reminiscent of those old Maytag commercials where the washing machine repairman had nothing to do.

"Can I help you"? He was alive.

"Yeah – I, uh –," and I proceeded to tell my tale. He put down the magazine and answered in a surprisingly articulate form of speech.

"Yes, it could very well be. It might need a new sensor."

"Can you just check that real quick"?

"No, I'd have to open it up and try a new one."

"Is it a big job"?

"Well, the sensor is about $25, labor – you're looking at about $75-80 – and you'd have to leave the set for 4 or 5 days." He went back to his magazine. My problem didn't seem too high on his priority list, in fact, I wondered if repairing anything appeared on his priority list. While pondering my next move, he caught me off guard with an unsolicited comment.

"What kind of TV is it"?

"Well, it's a 14" – ," as soon as I mentioned this numerical concept, that was it, game, set and match. He talked to me as if he were explaining something to a child.

"Hold it – we only fix big plasma TV's, sophisticated equipment, expensive stuff. You can go get a 14" color TV for $65-70, maybe even less, at Albertson's." He returned to his magazine. It seemed to be more his way of saying "get lost" than of enlightening himself.

I was stunned, not only for the price, but for the fact that they were selling TV's at Albertson's. I was speaking half to myself when I said, "Albertson's? The fresh food supermarket?" Without looking up, he nodded. Somehow, the whole cosmic balance seemed to be in doubt. They sell TV's in Albertson's. Where? Next to the romaine?

I pulled myself together and got serious. "Excuse me, **sir**"**!** My tone drew him away from the magazine. "I have a perfectly functioning, fairly new TV. Other than this sensor thing, there is nothing wrong with it. What am I supposed to do with it?"

He leaned forward and spoke sarcastically slow, "you – just – get – rid – of – it."

As I walked home, my confusion turned to anger. I remembered seeing a gross tee shirt on display in a store window that read, "Fuck you, you fucking fuck"! For me, the sale of such an item seemed no more gross than "you just get rid of it." In fact, they seemed to be close relatives in the emotional mindset of our culture. A genial idea dawned on me: maybe we should change the motto on our money from "In God We Trust" to "You Just Get Rid Of It." I finally had to break down and laugh under the weight of so much human stupidity.

Some of you out there in Essayland might be thinking that Post Consumer Man is being a bit hypocritical here, like, hey, why don't you just get up and change the channels?

It's a fair question.

Allow me to start my defense in a philosophical vein. It must be remembered that I am not in favor of blowing it all up, of returning to a pure state of nature, of starting all over again in a Gauguin-like flight from the lunacy of it all. I still believe, perhaps naively, in the use of technology. The Big Error is being perpetrated by our socio-economic model, a model that perverts the use of our technology, thus causing the eco-emotional madness which manifests itself in environmental degradation and a whole gamut of psychic lunacy, not the least of which being the latest spate of Bush Oil Wars (for more, see essays "The Unabomber," "The Economy," "Technology," "The Automobile," and others). It must be emphasized here that Post Consumer Man is not trying to lower your comfort level or drastically change your lifestyle. He is trying to propagate the idea that such comfort level could be accomplished with a microscopic amount of the industrial production we are currently drowning in. A person seated in front of a TV with a remote is not excluded from this concept.

But let's also get real here! The cable package I receive is far from the glitziest one, but it still starts at channel 2 and goes up into triple figures. A coast-to-coast trip across this vast viewing continent using the manual controls on the TV would be like crossing America in a covered wagon without roads. Anyone with the most minimal TV habit must have a remote. If this makes me an imperfect human being, so are you. So shut up!

Now I have to confront those think-tank, free market wonks who are going to tell us how great it is that you can buy something as sophisticated as a TV for only $70. "Look how great the system works." What they are not telling you is that the money you pay for that TV is not the only price being exacted. Take a look at the materials being used, the plastics, glass, metals, fusions and variations thereof. None of this grows on trees or can be picked up off the ground. A tremendous amount of both natural and human resources are being used to get that thing in front of your face.

And I'm supposed to "just get rid of it."

Look, I'm not a martyr. I'm not Mother Teresa. I've got a life to live and it is short enough. But there are hordes of people in the world living in squalor and misery.

And I'm supposed to "just get rid of it."

At least we can have some empathy for this situation. At least we can examine our own lives and try to understand its longer-range ramifications and how it fits into the global reality around us. You don't just throw away a car because the battery dies. The same principle should apply even for something that costs as little as a 14" color TV, which should be designed to repair minor glitches like a sensor malfunction cheaply and easily.

This is not a "bleeding heart" attitude. If we don't come to terms with these things, we are all going to pay a lot more later on.

WALMART
OR
THE STUPID ECONOMY

(10/08)

Any American with a moderate interest in politics will remember Bill Clinton's clever use of the phrase, "It's the economy, stupid," to keep his campaign for the presidency focused. As the years have gone by and my indulgence in economic ambiguity has deepened, I'd say the more proper phrase should be "It's the stupid economy, stupid." I am now firmly convinced it is just this particular economic system, currently tyrannizing humanity, that is the root cause of whatever negativity is assailing us. If it is not modified in a timely fashion, we will be, as they say over breakfast, "toast."

I was recently away from my natural habitat during my annual visit in the northern lairs of my birth. One of my siblings has a summer home about 3 hours north of Manhattan and a weekend trek has become a regular fixture. A Saturday night tradition has developed, one whereby 4 or 5 of us pile in the car and head for "town." Are we going to a restaurant, a movie, a few drinks, some partying – ?

Get real. We are going to Walmart.

Now, in order to protect my integrity – although I would not miss the chance to tag along – I never go with the intention of buying anything. But I must come clean: 2 years ago I found one of those 3 oz. bottles of Listerine I'd been looking for since the Carter administration. Its purchase brought joy to my life. Even PCM can be smitten with the shopping disease.

My main purpose in pursuing the Walmart experience is educational. I see it as a kind of anthropological expedition into the primitive culture of the global economy. There is much to learn in Walmart.

My previous trips to small town Walmart – all at this particular store, but there is a universal quality to the Walmart experience that precludes further reconnaissance – have given forth with a variety of impressions. My initial visit stood out for the Chick-Fillet restaurant operating within the store and the correspondent girth such industrial food has produced in the prototypical Walmart shopper. Put simply, there are a lot of fat people in Walmart. Other visits have demonstrated the moribund state of retail in close proximity to the huge invader. Some of it still has a weak pulse. Some of it is tumbleweed gone. None of it is pretty and much of this has been talked about in other forums.

What I'm about to say with regard to Walmart will not surprise most of you, although the quantification of the data could still be seen as useful. How I relate this data to the way in which our world functions is why this essay is taking form. It will show a perverse quality of the neo-liberal-global-economy that is rarely spoken about, unless you are traveling through the outer reaches of the

Blogosphere where few dare to tread. My recent Walmart experience, along with an anecdote a good friend recently related to me, helped bring this perversion into better focus for me, a perversion I'd like to bring into better focus for the vast majority of people who have probably never thought about it.

As is always the case, when my relatives scattered throughout the store in search of consumptive fulfillment, I began wandering around in search of the human condition. When I found myself in the "crappy plastic toy" section, which is a vast continent of soon to be broken artifacts meant to placate a child's boredom for a day or two, an inexplicable impulse to see where all this junk came from took hold of me. This section of the store is like a Nebraska cornfield stretching to the horizon. Thousands of shrill colored cardboard boxes with cellophane windows showing plastic monsters, tiny cars, mythical warriors, dump trucks, Barbie dolls, brigades of soldiers, cement mixers, ballet dancers, swords, daggers, scimitars, guns, rifles, water guns, bigger water guns, machine gun sets, houses, doggy puppets, fake cooking utensils – I could go on. After due deliberation, it can safely be said that 100% of all this schlock came from China. All of it. As my odyssey continued into other areas of the store, it soon became evident that the Chinese presence was never fully dormant, even if its omnipotence was not as dominant as in the "crappy plastic toy" section. In the clothing sections, although "made in China" was still noticeable, other very third world areas of the globe were more prevalent: India, Pakistan, Honduras, Egypt, El Salvador, Nicaragua, Bangladesh, Vietnam, Indonesia and others, all manufacturing things that used to be made in New England or the Piedmont regions of the American southeast. If we exclude foodstuffs, I'd say something like 75% of the merchandise in the store was made in China, and no more than 5% from the United States. Some big-ticket items like refrigerators, TV's and other electronic stuff, had their parts made in China but assembled in the United States. There was no instance of any merchandise made in any other country of the developed world. If we try to understand just how the global economy works, this is significant.

The only place that seemed to have a preponderance of American made goods was the firearms section. Some things are just too sacred to outsource – I guess.

Much of what has just been discussed has already been kicked around by other voices. We've heard about the loss of reliable, good paying manufacturing jobs; about the hardship this has caused, especially in small town America; about the general ripple effect of lower wages across the board; and even about the security threat such a diminished manufacturing base might entail. And then my good friend told me the anecdote mentioned above and a more lunatic aspect of all this became more obvious.

I'll call my friend Donald. As I write, the election season is in fifth gear. Due to his work, Donald occasionally delivers stuff to a man who is currently running for Sheriff in our county. He saw him the other day and struck up a conversation, the end of which being graced by the usual handshake. Unbeknownst to Donald, the candidate was holding something in his hand which he transferred to my friend's possession. With the usual display of patriotic symbolism our political candidates umbilically attach themselves to, it turned out to be a metallic sliver of an American flag with the candidate's name on it. Upon further examination, Donald saw that it was made in – you only get one guess.

The first thing one must remember is that this economically insignificant item, which requires no great know-how or special materials to make, is somebody's business. It was manufactured in order for someone to make money.

Fine. No problem there.

But have you ever stopped to think how ludicrous it is that the most economically feasible way to get this mundane American flag into the hand of my friend Donald began on the other side of the globe? It was manufactured, put in a truck container, sent to a seaport, put on a gigantic container ship, sailed across the vast expanse of the world's largest ocean, unloaded in another seaport, loaded onto another truck and distributed "from the gulf stream waters to the redwood forests," this metallic American flag was "made for you and me."

And yet, from a business standpoint, this was the most advantageous way to do it. Maybe I've lost my mind, but that seems a remarkable waste of resources just to sell a friggin' sliver of tin-plated American flag. There is only one kind of value system that could accept such monumental waste, and it is this neo-liberal-global-economy-capitalism now being rammed up our asses by the Rupert Murdochs of the world. The fact that this makes sense within the framework of this value system is living proof of how perverted it is. It is premised upon the fact that the labor of those in certain parts of the globe is given a worth somewhat close to zero. This is bad enough, but then think of the exaggerated amount of resources being used to accomplish this, and it begins to enter the realm of sinful in more than one way.

All these principles apply to the "crappy plastic toy" section and the rest of its kin in Walmart. What a "Rube Goldberg" has been mounted here, just to amuse junior for a day or two.

LIBERTARIANS

(2/11)

One of the great fads of American socio-economic thinking is currently living its salad days in the name of "libertarianism." I say "fad" because it is a philosophical concept inapplicable to the complex world we live in and cannot go beyond the rhetoric stage if a huge, technologically advanced, intricate society is to function. When it comes to libertarians, it is almost as if the expression "be careful for what you wish for" was coined with them in mind.

Let's start with the game of basketball. Perhaps none of our modern sports less resembles its origins than the contemporary game of basketball. If the sport's founder, Dr. Naismith, could have foreseen the pogo stick quality of today's players, he'd have hung his peach basket 5 feet higher. What was once a more controlled game played in closer harmony with gravity has now become a stampeding frenzy of gazelle-like acrobatics that has rendered my father's deadly two hand set shot to the scrap heap of history.

I can't speak for the game's most remote beginnings, but for almost the whole history of basketball the 2 man officiating crew was the norm. Then, about 20 years ago, the realization that the speed and tempo of the game had evolved to a point where 2 generally middle aged officials were having a hard time riding herd over the trampolining athleticism of the young impalas, became evident. Rather than waste the experience and know how of these battle tested officials, it was decided to add one more body to their crew, making 3 the norm.

I include this brief synopsis of basketball history in order to emphasize the absurdity of the libertarian point of view in an ever more crowded, fast moving, technologically connected, complex world. If we were to apply the libertarian idea to the sport of basketball, they'd have taken away one official. In fact! (Cue Howard Cosell) let's tell it like it is: they'd probably want to get rid of all the officials and let the players referee themselves.

How do you think that would work in Madison Square Garden?

These principles would apply to how a libertarian sees government. "Government" is another way to say how our whole socio-economic system is administered, or, if you may, refereed. The libertarian wants less and less refereeing, in spite of the fact that the game has changed exponentially since The Founders invented the country. Libertarians want to live by principles more applicable to colonial America than contemporary America.

Libertarians seem to ignore that almost all laws (all?) are a response to a heretofore unforeseen condition that has become problematic. If anyone out there can show me a law that anticipated a problem still to come, you know where to find me. Laws are responsive, not anticipatory. When automobiles were invented, their numbers were so minimal any rules pertaining to their use were inexistent. When they became more prevalent, it was evident this free for all had to end. Every time you stop at a red light or stop sign, you are giving up some freedom. When America was a sprawling, basically uninhabited place, you could homestead a piece of land, build a house and do whatever you damn well pleased with it. But guess what? Other people started to show up, housing tracts and residential neighborhoods began to form, and how would you like it if the guy next door opened a nightclub or body shop? Voila! Zoning laws. And then the industrial might of the nation went through puberty and grew into a strong, powerful being. This increased industrial capacity needed a place to dump its waste and the river we used to swim in began to take on diarrhea-like qualities. An important watershed was threatened. Holy crap! Environmental laws.

In each and every case, a law limiting our behavior became necessary. If the common good the law seeks to protect has more weight than the slither of freedom we relinquish to it, then it should be instituted. This does not mean all laws are good. Some are administered poorly, some are antiquated, some are not worth what they cost, and some are just plain bad ideas. But that is a function of good or bad government, which is a function of who the citizenry elects to govern them. It is not a function of whether we should or should not have laws. This is almost an issue that is mathematical in nature: the more complex a society is, the more administration it will need.

The current financial crisis the country is deeply mired in is a perfect example of this. Our most imposing private financial institutions were allowed to act in a reckless, even criminal manner (will somebody go see if William Holder, Esq., Attorney General of the United

States, is still on vacation). Starting from the days of St. Ronald of Hollywood, the biggest fraud ever deified by American folklore, the referees for this game were being systematically eliminated, until what was left was almost ceremonial. Who needs officials when that mirage-like concept known as the "market" can take care of it?

We all know the results of this policy and the myopic libertarians are correct in attacking the government, but they are doing it for the wrong reasons. They should not be attacking government as the problem; they should be attacking government for not doing its job! Meanwhile, the financial shysters at the tippy top of the economic pyramid, the ones responsible for this disaster, the ones for whom the government does not want to govern, are not even a remote blip on the libertarian radar screen.

These financial moguls must be laughing their butts off at the Bob Hope Country Clubs they hang out in.

It is difficult to talk about libertarians and not talk about taxes. A dose of gonorrhea is more palatable to a libertarian than the thought of paying taxes. There seems to be a disconnect here. The average libertarian will hop in the car, get out on the roads, cross a bridge here and there, send his kids to school, play a little ball on the softball field in the park, etc., etc., and somehow thinks this all exists through some kind of spontaneous generation. Now is the time to say the following: the citizens of the United States of America are not being overly taxed. As I've listened to the debates and discourse revolving around all the socio-economic issues now relevant in the United States and the world, it seems the most oft-used measure of tax burden is to compare the revenue raised against the Gross National

Product. As I write, you'd have to go all the way back to 1950 to find a moment in American history when the percentage of taxes paid was lower against GNP than it is now. Let me translate that – we paid more taxes in 1951 than we do now, and that was before Medicare!

You don't have to be a libertarian to legitimately question and complain about how our taxes are used and administered. It seems relevant for anyone to vociferously complain about who pays what (though the myopic libertarians don't seem to complain about that). But a libertarian is questioning the whole concept of taxation. In a complex, modern nation-state, that is just plain silly.

And that gets me where I'd like to go with this essay. I ask the reader to ponder the following question: what is the greatest accomplishment of modern capitalism? (Cue the music from the game show "Jeopardy").

"OK, your answer please."

An anguished contestant scrunches his face in thought – "What is – Viagra?"

Ooonnnkk! "No, I'm sorry. The correct answer is – the Social Contract or safety net it has been able to construct."

The fact that this system has created enough wealth so that a certain percentage of it can actually be set aside in a cooperative effort to provide the dignified minimal standard of life spoken about earlier in this work (see essay, "The Excrement Hits the Fan"), is a monumental accomplishment. If liberty and freedom is the Valhalla of a libertarian's mindset, their scorn for the government (people's) administered Social Contract is a grave error. Such things as universal health care, day care and pre-school, access to higher education through cheap loans and scholarships, old age pensions, minimum wages, housing subsidies, and other accouterments of such an idea, create more options in life for a vast block of society that would never have such opportunity. It weakens class barriers and encourages more social mobility. On the contrary, in a modern corporate environment, the libertarian idea does more to strangle freedom than enhance it. Its every man for himself attitude always creates an ever more concentrated mass of oligarchic wealth in fewer and fewer hands, a concept that is complemented by an ever increasing, generation to generation underbelly with less ability to defend its interests. In the end, the libertarian idea, in today's modern state, puts more people in shackles.

But I'll go even further. In so doing, I'll have to switch to the third person.

Over the course of the last few years, Post Consumer Man has been quite pragmatic in discussing the issues set forth by the financial crisis beginning in 2008. His thoughts, concepts, ideas and such have been confined to the framework of contemporary corporate capitalism because this is something that is not going away soon; this is where the bat hits the ball. However, when that last tweet is twittered on the I-phone of modern history, PCM's goal is to move us towards a new paradigm for life, one no longer based upon the idiotic, destructive incentives of the current economic system. As the years have gone by and this mass of dubious philosophical patter begins its flirtation with 1000 pages, PCM has never found a better word to describe the lunacy of our current socio-economic mindset than "consumerism." The Rube Goldberg qualities of a system whose only focus is the sale and possession of more and more superfluous "stuff," is creating an almost neurotic state we've begun to accept as normal. We've truly invented a monstrosity of colossal dimensions, a complex, overly complicated, tedious machine meant to accomplish the simple task of keeping us happy. The stress needed to maintain this machine is thwarting that goal.

And this is where a libertarian should become a brother of Post Consumer Man. If we could somehow (cue Jim Morrison) "break on through to the other side" and leave this adolescent stage of human development behind; if we could undo the exaggerated complexity the current economic system demands in playing the "consumerism" game; if we could develop more mature, spiritual incentives for human fulfillment, the libertarian idea becomes a more harmonious bi-product of such. In such a world, government can become that odorless, colorless liquid a libertarian might relate to. It becomes an anonymous administer of the Earth's resources, rather than a vehicle for ambition and greed in a hyper-material world. If libertarians want less of a role for government, they should think of themselves a "post-consumerists" rather than libertarians.

What libertarians don't seem to understand is that their creed cannot exist in harmony with the complex subterfuges of corporate capitalism. You cannot have one with the other. But in a "post-consumerist" world –

Welcome aboard.

THE HISTORY OF CAPITALISM

(10/11. This is the second in a series beginning with "The Occupation of Wall Street")

As mentioned in the previous essay, the spontaneity of the "Occupy" movement has unleashed a protest with an ambiguous personality. Many different elements of grievance have coalesced in these demonstrations including wealth distribution, money in politics, anti-war sentiment, ecological concerns, civil rights and other micro-focal points of unrest all galvanized in a macro protest against a socio-economic system millions of people have lost faith in. Most of all, people feel as if they are getting <u>screwed</u> and there is no one there, in a supposedly democratic system, to represent them. Here they are, being victimized by a financial crisis they did not cause while those sitting 50 floors above in their glittering skyscrapers, people who do not produce a product, people who do not service, repair or maintain anything, people who do little more than manipulate numbers in a balance sheet shell game that somehow leaves them with tens of millions of dollars in personal wealth, all this, while the rest of us barely survive working for a living. Perhaps this whole movement can be summed up in the words of the great football coach, Vince Lombardi: "what the hell is going on here"?

So what we have, at this point, is an instinctive uprising against a tyrannical force that is hard to define. There is no Mubarak here. The protesters themselves are not un-American, they are not dogmatic Communists or Socialists, they are not radicals. They generally believe in the America they were taught to love, but they see that America being phased out of existence. They are protesting, but that is the easy part. The hard part is to define what you want.

I will now define what it is these protesters want. That might seem a presumptuous thing to do, but I write with the full confidence that what I'm about to say will find an almost unanimous state of acceptance amongst the "Occupiers."

Although demonstrations of this nature find it "politically correct" to deny political affiliation of any kind, there is always something political in play when ideas are involved. It is possible to shun existing political formations, but political ideology cannot be avoided when protest for or against anything is involved. Whatever you are against, whatever you are for, falls somewhere on the political ideological landscape.

These demonstrators, whether they can articulately express it to themselves or anyone else, are clamoring to re-establish the traditional center-left or liberal ideal that has been so maligned and eaten away at since the appearance in America of my favorite "axis of evil," Ronald Reagan and Rupert Murdoch. A logical addendum to this idea is to rebuild the ideological foundation of a

Democratic Party that has been ripped off its foundation and floundering, mainly due to the financial pressures of competing in the current political system. Although the target of this liberal ideology includes a varying array of goals, its bulls-eye is the idea of a social safety net or Social Contract between its citizens, one that can provide a dignified minimal living standard for as many people as possible. This primal, fundamental goal of liberalism dovetails quite readily with other policy concerns such as an anti-militarism that could free up immense amounts of resources for other things, civil rights and equality issues, wealth distribution, etc. But the bull's- eye, I repeat, is a strong Social Contract-safety net that is the underpinning for everything else.

In order to make this point, I'd like to give a brief class in modern capitalism. In so doing, I will put forth 3 basic assertions that corroborate the idea that this Social Contract or safety net is the true goal of these protests.

1) <u>The greatest single triumph of modern capitalism is, precisely, this social safety net.</u> The raw fact that this socio-economic system can produce such gargantuan amounts of wealth so that a reasonable percentage of it can be reclaimed and recycled through the system for the common good is a spectacular accomplishment. In fact, it is the latest socio-political evolutionary step towards a more fulfilled human condition, and history tells us it can be done without ruining the creativity and incentives for money making that characterize capitalism in general.

There are a variety of mechanisms that can be used to fund and form the communal well being the Social

Contract represents. Obviously, taxation is a formidable tool here and a fair and just levy against personal wealth and business profits is an essential source of revenue. But there are also sales taxes, tolls, fees for licenses, permits and other bureaucratic necessities, fees to use public facilities and such that even the humblest citizen (and non-citizen) pays into. But taxation is not the only game in town. Governmental administration of the private sector, that is, proper oversight and regulation that maintains a healthy competitive balance that, in the long run, creates a more profitable wealth creation mechanism, is another tool for the propagation of a society that can afford a social safety net. This also includes vigilant mechanisms for the rights of workers and their ability to defend their interests – unions, safety, unemployment insurance, sick leave, etc. All this conspires, if done properly, in creating a healthy economic engine whose wealth can be administered in a way that benefits the most people.

Such things as day care, school food programs, good public education, affordable higher education, pensions, public recreation facilities, minimal wage flooring, and a whole host of Social Contract services, including the biggest Kahuna of all and the source of America's greatest shame, a proper health care system, are not hand outs. Social Security is not a hand out. Medicare is not charity. Almost all people participate in the wealth-creating machine of the capitalist system. The guy working on a loading dock at Walmart is creating wealth. The Latino woman mopping the floors in a skyscraper is creating wealth. Their paychecks cannot be considered the only remuneration they have earned. They also earn a dignified minimal standard of life with their labor. That is what the social safety net is for.

Perhaps the most vivid way I can make this argument is to say 2 things: a) a rich man's wealth would be meaningless without this army of people below doing so many things to provide his lifestyle, and b) when a rich man starts complaining about how this or that group is getting a hand out, or jobbing the system, or getting something for nothing; when this rich man starts acting as if this poor man is swindling him, ask him if he'd like to trade places with him.

2) A post Industrial Revolution capitalist system without a social safety net is a failure. You can look it up. This unfettered, unregulated, purely market driven form of the beast – what the Europeans call "savage capitalism" – was what developed from its catalytic root, the Industrial Revolution. This is the kind of world writers like Charles Dickens and Sinclair Lewis were looking at. It created huge amounts of wealth, but it did not create a better human condition. This is the kind of world the socialist ideologues of the late 19th and early 20th centuries were looking at. People like Marx and Bakunin were correct in their analysis of an economic system that was horribly exploitive of the very many by a pathetic few; of a system that created huge amounts of poverty and degradation in a world of plenty; of a system that perpetrated these conditions with a minimal amount of social mobility.

We might call this era of capitalist history its "immature" stage and it didn't reach puberty until the Great Depression changed the game. We might say it had to grow up and become more reasonable if it were to meet the challenges of the 20th century. This immature kind of capitalism is what right wing elements of wealth and power have always tried to maintain throughout the whole history of modern capitalism. With the help of the economic clout of their wealth, most embodied in the ability to control the political system in America and evangelized by huge private sector media voices, many people whose interests don't coincide with these right wing elements are always duped into following them (hello, Tea Party). For the last 30 years or so, America, and to a lesser extent the whole world, has been drifting back towards this immature capitalism.

Look where it has gotten us.

3) <u>It was the more highly evolved or grown up form of capitalism, the one that developed a social safety net, which defeated Communism</u>. In fact, it might even be said the social safety net itself defeated Communism. Although the immature form of capitalism "muckraked" by people like Dickens and Lewis propagated huge amounts of wealth, it also created misery in unacceptable levels. Its negative aspects actually spawned the Communist reaction to it. Wealth creation alone was not the answer.

An American could proudly say that Franklin Roosevelt, in his necessary attempts to deal with the Great Depression (we can thank the immature form of capitalism for that), was the father of the social safety net idea. I'd give some credence to that assertion, but the concept truly bloomed and reached fruition in the rebuilt Europe after WWII. The first Labor governments in

England immediately after the war, led by such figures as Harold Wilson and Harold MacMillan, could be considered the triggers of the Social Contract idea, but the rest of western Europe was either not far behind or doing the same things. The various forms of universal health care are triumphant legacies of this "grown up" form of capitalism.

Although only the United States could defend the capitalist idea militarily, the western Europeans were in the front lines in defending its ideology. Its social safety net provided a better standard of living for its working class than the Soviets did in their "worker's paradise." It was able to do so because, if managed properly, it did not compromise the capitalist wealth-making machine. The immature form of capitalism in place before WWII might not have withstood the Communist idea, an idea that was an altruistic reaction to the failures of "savage capitalism."

With the fall of the Soviet Union, the conservative elements of the market system, that is, those controlling vast amounts of wealth at the tip of its economic pyramid, those who have always opposed the expense of the social safety net in a short sighted, counter productive (even for their interests) attempt to preserve even more wealth for themselves, have been flexing their muscles. They've been getting their way for quite some time now, and they've brought us to the brink of another Great Depression.

The time has come to stop them.

So class, let's review the day's work: 1) the greatest accomplishment of capitalism is the social safety net. 2) Capitalism without the social safety net is a failure. 3) It is just this social safety net that defeated Communism.

The sooner the "occupy" movement can recognize this as the foundation of their demands, the sooner it can become a viable political force for change.

A Post Script from Post Consumer Man – *Post Consumer Man would like to remind the reader that he is neither a capitalist nor communist nor anything in between. He chooses not to define himself in such terms. He has transcended these ideological concepts by referring to himself as a "Post-Consumerist." A Post Consumerist sees the folly of the hyper-consumptive necessities of our current economic system and considers such mega-consumption the root of all problems mankind is now confronting. A Post Consumerist believes that by providing for our material needs in a more mature, rational way, we can provide for our more important emotional needs in a more satisfying way. For Post Consumer Man, not even the optimal form of capitalism just described in this essay is the answer. But –*

– if we are to move on, to transcend it, to evolve higher as a species, this optimal form of capitalism could be the bridge to the future. When the most people can be given a dignified standard of life, one where the struggle to survive does not monopolize one's efforts, new ideas, new outlooks, the search for "better" in an environment of intellectual curiosity, find more fertile ground to grow in.

In other words, if we look at it as a stop along the way and not as an end in itself, this optimal form of capitalism is the only thing a Post Consumerist can advocate for in a world still not ready to leave "consumerism" behind.

PESSIMISM

(4/12)

I've been writing these essays for something like 20 years now and I'm proud to say the output of such is approaching 1000 pages of self perceived wisdom gathered in hundreds of essays (what others perceive is an open question). In truth, it is not a remarkable amount of material for a person postulating oneself as a writer-philosopher. However, although I consider this work the axel around which the wheel of my life revolves, it pays no bills, thus obliging me to render much time to an unrelated job of little import. Given these circumstances, the yield can be seen as a constant, if not overwhelming quantity of work that demonstrates a true desire to communicate a point of view, one in direct conflict with a cultural status quo possessed of a gargantuan communications apparatus capable of drowning out all resistance.

I am Post Consumer Man and although I do not stand alone, such voices sparsely populate the landscape in the same way a few water holes might dot a huge desert. We are voices of dissidence, voices that have been so obliterated by the consumer society's sound machine that we pose no threat and perhaps never will. There are no "Gulags" necessary. We seem to be losing.

Pessimism.

If a "Post Consumerist" believes that the absurd consumptive demands of our current economic system are the catalyst for every problem now assaulting the flora and fauna of existence – and remember, such consumption is not a choice but a necessity for this system's survival – then how do we make our dissidence more palpable, more acceptable, more possible?

For anyone with a fresh socio-political vision, the desired goal is to evolve methodically towards the longed for new "paradigm" with as little apocalyptic upheaval as possible. This kind of emotional growth could be considered the definition of civilized behavior. Unfortunately, more often than not the lessons of history have taught us that the significant socio-cultural advancements of humanity are generally procured in an atmosphere of belligerence and great suffering. If, as Post Consumer Man sees it, the goal is to get us beyond this adolescent model of frivolous consumption, the prospects for it being done in the civilized manner mentioned above seem dim indeed. To think those with the greatest vested interests in the consumer society would ever objectively allow us into a new reality not imprisoned by the consumptive necessities of the current system, is akin to believing in the tooth fairy. What makes a "Post Consumerist's" outlook even more pessimistic is the subtle way the consumer society invokes its propaganda.

The vast majority of neo-liberal capitalism's political propaganda is camouflaged as commercial propaganda and its message is as incessant as surf pounding the shore.

Most people do not think of the commercials they see and hear everyday as political propaganda, but one foolish enough to give some thought to the question (guilty) comes to realize they are inseparable. The political message facilitates the commercial message and vice versa. But it is this daily carpet-bombing of commercial persuasion that is most responsible for the cultural (and political) mindset of the consumer society. It is the most intrusive and thorough form of mind control the world has ever seen, and yet, most people believe their free will is unadulterated. This is how first rate propaganda works.

This is what a "Post Consumerist" is up against.

In spite of the pessimism with which I see the future, I cannot be defined as a depressed person. Anyone who knows me can attest to the fact that I generally interact with my place in the grand scheme of things in a reasonable way. And yet, there are times when my pessimism is nudged into that more hard-bitten, extreme version of it known as "hopelessness." This is a more dangerous emotional state and 2 recent incidents in my life put me there for awhile.

Not too long ago I was hired to drive two elderly gentlemen to Fort Lauderdale. It had been maybe 30 years since I'd last been there and although I've never been fond of the urban style of south Florida, this updated version could be described as horrifying. From horizon to horizon stretched a panorama of pavement, poured concrete, strip malls, glass encrusted office buildings and a general permeation of plastic-neon anti-nature, all serviced by the veins and arteries of newly constructed but never quite completed freeways, interstates, turnpikes and 6 lane local conduits crawling with the mechanical insects of slowly moving motor vehicles all "hurrying" to somewhere they were probably late for. It was a huge savannah of sterility, almost desert-like in its complete denial of whatever natural landscape might have existed there before the coming of the global economy. As I try to recollect the experience, I simply cannot visualize a tree, a bush, or anything vegetable appearing in this concrete desert, although I'm sure there had to be a botanical presence somewhere, even if it hardly registered in the human consciousness. What I was looking at was a hip-hop sneer of habitat destruction and species annihilation. What was that novel – was it Mary McCarthy? – which explained it wasn't God that was dead; it was nature that was dead.

The gentlemen I was working for were excellent companions, which made our presence in this "foreign land" a more bearable endeavor, especially since we were temporary intruders rather than habitual inhabitants of the daily traffic jam we found ourselves lodged in. My negative epiphany occurred while barely moving in the strangling vehicular mass of a highway with a speed limit of 60 mph. As we crept across an overpass an almost complete vista of modern Fort Lauderdale assaulted our senses. In an act of pure spontaneity, I began thinking out loud. "It's moments like this when I begin to feel utterly defeated, when I realize this has caught hold of us in an irreversible way, that there is no other reality to turn to, that our concepts of fulfillment or happiness or whatever, are in the jail of this mind set. It's moments like this when I begin to realize there is no turning back and the consequences of such will have to be suffered somewhere down the line – and it won't be pretty."

This is more than pessimism.

The other incident occurred during my annual jaunt to Miami to see one of the world's most important tennis tournaments. Over the years, I've come to realize that the lure of watching these spectacular athletes is little more than the "come on" in a more serious game, that being the selling of merchandise. This is where the real money is. The athletes are paid mythical amounts to be the bait on the hook the consumer-tennis fan will bite. Their athletic talent has landed them well-paid jobs as models for the apparel, shoes, racquets, timepieces, tennis bags, accessories and paraphernalia of all stripes. This is the business of tennis, of Wall Street, of the global economy in general, and the athletic talent is little more than the showroom for a more serious reach into your wallet.

Listen up Mr. and Mrs. Tennis fan: your primary role in this whole fandango is not to watch tennis or to be a fan. That is just a smokescreen. What they really want from you is to buy stuff, more stuff, the latest stuff, the stuff that replaces the stuff they got you to buy 3 months ago. You are no different than a nicotine addict. You are hooked.

My negative epiphany occurred while walking the grounds of the tournament site, an extended piece of real estate containing practice courts, the 16 courts for tournament play, a stadium court holding 15 thousand shoppers, and a sprawling midway of culinary choices, beverages both soft and hard and – cue the trumpets! – merchandise tents representing all the great labels in the sporting world.

Perhaps the biggest installation was the Adidas facility, a super market sized extravaganza teeming with its latest line of shirts, shoes, shorts, pants, skirts, caps, socks, jackets, visors and who knows what else. I decided to enter the tent for educational purposes, as if I were an anthropologist studying the primitive culture of 21st century consumerism (where's Margaret Meade when you need her?). What I found was an almost hysterical atmosphere, a kind of feeding frenzy of consumption, like hyenas gleefully gorging themselves on the carcass of a fallen wildebeest. The crowds were dense and hard to maneuver in, an inconvenience gone totally unnoticed by the hungry hyena-shoppers. A feeling of ecstasy filled the air as the herd sifted its way through the merchandise. The 5 or 6 lines leading to the cashiers were 10 deep with people clutching their latest purchases as if they were dearly beloved infants.

For Post Consumer Man, standing in the shopping hurricane raging all around him, his feeling of alienation received its "coup de grace" in the words of a nearby teen age girl speaking to her friend. "I love this, I love it, I don't ever want to leave."

And now, more than a week has gone by and the hopelessness spawned by my foray into the heartbeat of the consumer society has returned to its more manageable state of pessimism. With my mind in its more routine mode, the objections to this rant now become impossible to ignore and the primary one would seem to be this:

"But Post Consumer Man, it seems this is what human beings want. As you say, they love it, it motivates them, they can't get enough of it."

True, this can't be denied. There seems to be some kind of nerve, or fiber, or convolution in our brains that seeks these material rewards. But the consumer culture – and by this I mean the economic system that demands this behavior – has decided to stimulate this nerve not just to its maximum, but almost to the exclusion of everything else. This is not a natural act. One must remember the hyenas in the Adidas tent already have tons of this "stuff" in their closets. They don't need the things they will be buying today or tomorrow. They want it for purely emotional reasons they have been inculcated (brainwashed?) into artificially.

"But Post Consumer Man, so what? What's the harm, let them have their fun."

No. Their attitude is a destructive one (see essay, "Destructive People"). The system's rewards are not worth the aggravation it is causing – economically, sociologically, ecologically, politically, etc. Its end game could be very ugly.

Is anyone listening?

Pessimism.

I KNOW YOU'RE LISTENING

(6/13, Spain. This is the second of 2 starting with "The Spaniards Take Notice")

Dear CIA-FBI Guy,

Being that you are listening to everything I and everyone else in my country is saying, I thought I'd have a chat with you, as long as I have you on the line. Let's get one thing straight before continuing: I do not resent you, or hate you, or even dislike you. What I feel for you is something more like pity. A job like yours can only be had when you've convinced someone just as pitiful as you of your unquestioned loyalty and dedication. People like you are not just my-country-right-or-wrong people, you are people who cannot even imagine your country ever being wrong. There is a fanaticism in your belief that, ironically, is not that different from the Taliban-Al Queda-Shabazz-Shabamm people who've rattled this country to such an extent, we've forgotten who we are and what we supposedly stand for. Being a fanatic or true believer like an Islamist terrorist, or someone like you, spying on millions of your fellow citizens, always entails a certain degree of naivety and simple thinking. It is evident to me, Mr. CIA-FBI Guy, regardless of the time and place in history you were born into, you'd be doing the same thing for whatever propaganda device you lived under, be it Hitler's racial utopia, Stalin's worker's paradise, Franco's pious Catholic beatitude, as well as America's supposedly free and democratic mercantile despotism, which is where the roulette wheel of your birth deposited you. Your ability to think for yourself has either never existed or was easily erased by the demagoguery you've so easily fallen for.

I find that pitiful.

As I'll explain later on, I am even more dangerous to your precious American way of life than any Islamic terrorist could ever be, even though I've never committed an act of physical aggression on anyone, nor do I ever plan to. I've never so much as touched a real firearm, something, I suppose, that makes me a suspicious character, *ipso facto*, in today's America.

Perhaps by now you've made contact with a superior, like hey, we might have a live one here, a true threat to our national security, I better tell someone fast. The ironic part is that you could be right, but for all the wrong reasons. As you know, my name is not Abdul or Youseffe, I'm not a "towel head" or "sand nigger," I'm not only not a Moslem, I don't believe in their god, or your god, or my god, my god! when will humanity stop using that word, can't we ever get past this simple minded way to explain ourselves to each other? And I hope your boss has showed up by now, so I can pity him as well, pity him for being so afraid of a handful of religious fanatics, so afraid that he is willing to compromise the finest aspects of his country in the name of – get this – freedom!

Hey, Mr. CIA-FBI Guy, have you ever stopped to think how for almost 50 years we stared down an opposing empire with a military apparatus equal to ours, a military apparatus the likes of which the world had never known, without fanatics like you having to listen to whatever I was saying or communicating? We won WWII. We won the Cold War. We survived numerous threats to our sovereignty and way of life, without anyone having to listen in on the puny little life of someone like me.

Guess what? I'm getting hungry. Why don't you and anyone else who might be listening come back in about a half an hour, when we can resume this "unilog"? Maybe we can save some taxpayer money, especially in these times of "austerity," something that perhaps does not affect you guys, who seem to be part of the one sector of our economy that is experiencing growth, that being the "espionage sector."

Ahh, that hit the spot; toasted bagel with some all-natural, vegetable-based butter – gee, maybe I shouldn't have said that. It sounds kind of subversive, doesn't it? Write that down, Mr. CIA-FBI Guy: he could be a vegetarian in addition to an atheist who's never touched a firearm.

Perhaps you guys went out and got a Big Mac with fries, as any good American would, but I doubt it. To leave your post for a half an hour in times of such danger to the "homeland" would be a dereliction of duty our intelligence units – forgive me, sorry for the sardonic cackling, but every time I hear that word "intelligence" used in reference to people like you, it cracks me up.

You guys are like Pavlovian dogs, conditioned to act in a very narrow way. My country! My light in the darkness of the enemies all around us – forgive me once again. You guys should have been comedians. I may be laughing on the outside, but it is no joke. You actually believe you are defending the country, its democracy, its freedom, its liberty – Holy cow! Mr. CIA-FBI Guy, you are actually being paid with my tax dollars to listen to me! A Mr. Nobody! A Miami Marlins fan! Could anything be more innocent than that? Could anything be more totalitarian than that?

Listen up. I'm getting to the part that explains why I am a much more serious threat than all the Osama Bin Bejesuses out there, fanatically defending their cause in the same way you are.

Without you really knowing it, what you are defending is a global corporate dictatorship. You don't really work for your country. That is just a cover for a totalitarian economic system that is omnipresent all over the world. Your country's "democratic government" is no more than the political wing of the Corporate Dictatorship, just as Sein Finn was for the IRA, or Hamas is for some of the terrorists you are so afraid of. You work for the few "illuminati" that control the colossal scam of neo-liberal capitalism. Much more so than a country, you defend an economic system, one that is strangling the world in all the diverse problems caused by what has now become known as "consumerism."

Mr. CIA-FBI Guy, did you ever think just why it is we've gotten into this shit with the Ayrabs? Did you ever stop to think how much oil is needed to feed the absurd appetite for energy the Corporate Dictatorship you work for demands? Maybe if you got your finger out your ass and read a few of Post Consumer Man's essays, one like "Destructive People," or "Pessimism," or "Post Consumer

Man," you'd have a better idea of what I'm talking about. There is no need to secretly listen in on my life, to be hiding in some clandestine bunker living on Chinese take out, so stuck up with yourself and your mission to save your country. Just go to postcman.info and educate yourself. Stop being a stooge in a silly movie.

I won't hold my breath, but as long as I have you on the line, I'll try and make it as simple as I can, in deference to the constipated scope of your thinking.

The true tyranny in the world is the economic system itself, the economic system you so blindly work for. Although your bosses would have us believe our behavior affects the economic system, it is really the other way around: the economic system affects our behavior. In order for it to work as it should, it demands this behavior and does everything within the vast scope of its persuasionary apparatus to make us "consumers" behave this way. In order for the economic system to work as it should, that is, so that the whole montage does not fall apart, we must be consuming in a way that is so preposterous, it becomes a negative force in the world; it becomes the catalyst for everything gone wrong. But the frightening part is this: we cannot opt out! There is no "freedom" to do so. We are enslaved to an economic system that is doing great harm. Mr. CIA-FBI Guy, you are not working for our freedom, you are working for our enslavement!

And here is where me, Post Consumer Man, comes in. This is where you have to listen real good if you want to defend your country and its "way of life." If you want to go get a superior further up the chain of command, I'll give you 15 minutes while I go take a dump. This would be a good time for you and anyone else documenting this "unilog" to do the same.

Ahh, nothing like a good bowel movement to get one back in the action, eh, Mr. CIA-FBI Guy? I hope you're refreshed and ready because this is the big news; this is why the real subversive – "terrorist," if you may – is me, not some falafel-faced fanatic spewing forth his hate so uselessly. And here's why:

I've opted out.

Ah-hah! you might think, with the minimal amount of deductive capacity you still possess, you contradicted yourself there, you said we are slaves, that we can't opt out, and now you're whistling a different Dixie, ah-hah, we got you –

Yes, Mr. CIA-FBI Guy, I've opted out, but there are still so few of us we pose no threat to the Corporate Dictatorship you spy for. We are like those few wolverines living in the inhospitable snowy wastes above the tree line, surviving in what is left of a healthy environment for us. However, if we defer to the true reality of things, if this economic system you defend, along with the adolescent behavior it demands, is to survive, we can't opt out, and you can bet your Lehman Brothers portfolio the people you are spying for will do everything in their immense powers to keep us in the fold. The fact that they've lost me and a few others is still so inconsequential they have not been forced to erase us – yet.

By now, Mr. CIA-FBI Guy, if my grasp of your intellectual ability is correct, you might be scratching your head and thinking, "opt out of what?" Dude, I don't buy stuff. They shoot commercial messages at me day after day, week after week, year after year, all day, all night, and it has no effect. I've quit buying. I've redefined my idea of fulfillment and it is not your boss's definition of it. This is dangerous. Compared to me, the boys of Islam are a barely perceived blemish on the big fat butt of the global economy, an unfortunate but peripheral annoyance for the brokers of "consumerism." Compare that to the real threat caused by me, Post Consumer Man, and the other wolverines out there who've cracked the code and see the unbalanced negativity caused by an economic system whose rewards are becoming less and less effective in combating the collateral damage it is causing.

You should be frightened to death of us wolverines, frightened that what we understand could ever find traction amongst the vast herd of lemmings you unconsciously herd over the cliff. We'd be invincible. You cannot throw people in jail for not wanting yet another new Nike creation for Roger Federer. You cannot persecute someone for not needing a new car. You'd be helpless before an idea of immense significance. Not only that, a post consumptive society would no longer need your services. You'd have to find a job; an honorable job, a productive job, not this inquisitional-Torquemada task our society is currently squandering its resources on.

So you better come and get me now, before this kind of subversive thinking catches on. Nip it in the bud. You know where I live, shit, by now you probably know when I jerk off, so come and get me. My door is always open. I live comfortably but have virtually nothing worth stealing. I'll be expecting you. I'll go peacefully. I've never so much as touched a firearm –

PART II

POLITICS, GOVERNMENT, THE BURLESQUE OF THOSE IN CHARGE

SPY VS. SPY

(This essay was written in the mid 90's. I can't remember for sure, but I think the American spy involved in this fiasco was named Walker. Considering the fear and paranoia that has become the currency of George W.'s popularity, its relevance in America 2005 makes it worth posting here.)

One of the big stories hitting the newsstands as I write is a scandal involving a CIA agent who allegedly passed information to the Soviets and continued to do so now that they are simply the Russians. The fact that the Russians, who are now deemed our "friends" by those creating such images, have continued to spy, sneak and try to get the drop on us, has angered a significant amount of patriots. A varying array of politicos and cellular phone VIP's have lobbied to keep the "Big Mac" out of Moscow, along with other punitive actions that would limit the introduction of our technology and superior good looks into a nation that continues to do such weaselly things. It has been suggested that we should not, at this delicate juncture in the two country's tri-lateral relations, teach the Russians how to throw a curve ball, especially since they learned to shoot jump shots and slap shots much better than we ever wanted them to.

This initial call for swift castigation soon began to waiver. Everyone knows that nobody trusts their wives anymore, and everyone is spying on everyone else, friend or foe, and that a "cheap and secure supply of oil" is all that matters anyway (see essay "Christians").

But something had to be done.

As a result, the President, he of the "stupid economy" (see essay "The Economy"), decided to deport an Armenian janitor working in the Russian embassy, accusing him of selling caviar to White House staff that turned out to be nothing more than fish eggs. He was put on the first plane to Newark and then driven immediately to Jersey City, where he was put out and told never to return to the United States again.

Judging from the media coverage (how else can we judge?), this seems to have been a very big deal. Even the President, gravely holding sway at a hastily called press conference, considered it "very serious." While watching it on TV, I had an uncontrollable urge to get up and lock my door. Who can you trust these days?

This is not the first time something like this has happened. Such stories seem to dance across our collective consciousness every four or five years, once again exposing the clever, sinister qualities of our enemies and just how vulnerable our recipes for the perfect barbecue sauce really are. It is alleged that our whole intelligence gathering apparatus has been rendered useless ... again! It has raised grave questions as to the efficiency and effectiveness of the CIA ... again! How is it that the "Russkies" have gotten over on us ... again! What to do?

Given the fact that the United States is the world's most powerful and prestigious nation, the one who the rest of the clods look to in order to lead humanity on towards whatever disasters might lie ahead, while the old Soviet Union lies fractured and dismantled, seemingly incapable of manufacturing a paper clip without our help, I say we leave the CIA exactly the way it is. We seem to have stumbled upon something here – the worse spies we have, the better off we get. I recommend Maxwell Smart for the head job at the CIA. As long as some double agent doesn't sell this valuable state secret to the "Russkies," the "Japs," the "Krauts," or the Uzbekistanis (the Uzis?), we will continue to lead the free, kind of free, ball busted and pussy whipped world.

It must be clear by now that I don't take this affair as seriously as the President does. For a working stiff like myself, who drags his ass out of bed at forgotten hours in an effort to nourish, clothe and put a roof over his aching, over-the-hill body, such subterranean worlds of sleuthery, treachery, and 00 theatrics are about as relevant as galoshes in the Sahara Desert. Am I to believe that continuing screw ups in this shrouded dimension of airports, embassies and unknown capital cities will eventually mean the end of a culture where people in laughably ugly red and blue shirts deliver pizzas at all hours of the night, the first two toppings magnanimously given free of charge? Hey man, spring training is about to start. Don't these spies have something better to do?

If there is one thing that jumps out at me in examining this matter, it's the alleged perpetrator's motivation for his betrayal. Like almost all Americans who have done something like this, his acts were not ideologically inspired. During the early Cold War era, British intelligence was rocked by the betrayals of some of its most talented and highly placed agents. Unlike their American counterparts, they were motivated by altruistic reasons. They were socialists and believed in the cause. Contrast this to our latest "Benedict Arnold," who, like other American traitors, did it for the money. He and his wife bought a beautiful new home in suburbia. They purchased an elegant Jaguar. They probably wanted a Jaguar all their lives. They started living the "American Dream." What could be more American than that?

If this guy is considered subversive, then I'm Che Guevara.

GERALD R. FORD: HE'S DEAD

(1/07. This essay could be read as the second part of a series starting with the essay "Milhous," where Gerald Ford was first mentioned.)

When it comes to presidential anonymity, such names as Taylor, Milliard F., Rutherford B. and Buchanan come to mind (is that a contradiction in terms?). But it might not be fair to compare such pre-electronic history with our wired 20th century leaders. With this in mind, it is comfortable to say that the most anonymous, faceless, forgettable president in the last 100 years was Gerald R. Ford. That is –

until he died.

Now that he is dead, and with the help of our ever-vigilant free press, the truth is finally coming out, a reality that was shrouded in secrecy for the nation's own good. In one of the best-kept secrets in the Republic's history, it has now been revealed that Gerald R. Ford was perhaps the greatest president we ever had. In fact, he could even be described as a martyr.

With the great advantage of his death, we can now begin to see that the time frame encompassed by Ford's 2 plus years in office called for a purely distilled form of mediocrity he brought to fruition with something bordering on perfection. Gerald Ford had a keen instinct for the mediocre that made him the perfect man at just the time America needed such qualities the most.

And we all thought he was just another political hack. Who knew?

In the wake of the Nixon Watergate scandals, with the country staggering under the weight of the first president in its history forced to resign for criminal activities, the best course of action, with hindsight, was a president who could attract as little attention as possible, someone who could take our minds off the presidency, someone who could disappear into the foliage of the political forest with hardly a trace.

I mean, hey, we don't want to know from presidents for awhile. Just go away.

One has to believe that God truly blessed America with the appearance of Gerald R. Ford to do just that.

Now that Ford is dead, and the truth of his perfectly disguised brilliance is finally coming out, one has to wonder if the mediocrity he so appropriately gave the nation was just an accidental twist of fate that fortuitously befell us all, or if he shrewdly realized such a lack of talent and creativity was just what the historical context of the moment called for? In other words, and in spite of the fact that he conned us into thinking he was a useless sap, did he instinctively know the mediocrity of a forgettable presidency was necessary in saving the nation, and did he, with all the genius he so naturally hid, purposely create an atmosphere that not only made the office he held invisible, but even loveable once again?

Now that he is dead, and we are finally finding out that his presidency was perhaps the greatest of all time, I tend to believe the latter, and I offer the following incident to make my point:

Before describing said incident, it is relevant to note that President Ford was a great athlete, being a fine football player at the University of Michigan, where he played in the Rose Bowl. Not even his deft attempts to hide his talents under a forgettable pall of averageness could obliterate his athletic gifts. This well-known fact of President Ford's life ties in with the now to be described, aforementioned incident.

Before President Ford was dead, when his true greatness was still being denied our access, the only thing I remember from his life was an event that took place during his presidency. His plane had just landed in some European capital in one of those typically dank, drizzly days on the old continent. As is customary in these moments, the main hatch swung open and the president appeared at the top of the stairway. After a momentary smile and greeting, he began his descent and immediately slipped and fell on the first step, bouncing his ass perfectly off each successive step until it found its resting place unceremoniously on the tarmac. Bum-bum-bum-bum-bum-bum – plop! Absolutely gorgeous.

Now that he is dead, and we are just beginning to comprehend the magnificent method behind this seemingly incompetent façade of mediocrity, it is easy to see that president Ford staged this memorable moment (and, to his credit, in his marvelous attempt to deflect attention away from a suffering executive branch, it is the only event most of us can remember from his administration). One is led to believe this for 2 reasons: 1) would an athlete of his stature be so clumsy as to end up in such a ridiculous situation, and, 2) could anyone but an athlete of his stature have carried it out with such "panache," "savoir faire" and "chutzpah"? C'mon, we all know the answers here. President Ford, in his attempts to look like the inoffensive bumpkin the president needed to be after the tortured reign of Richard Nixon, sacrificed his persona and his butt in order to save the nation. I'm sure I speak for all Americans everywhere in expressing our sadly belated gratitude.

But that was not enough self sacrifice for this, up until now, unappreciated genius and singular American public servant.

Now that he is dead, and with our diligent watchdogs in the media refreshing our memories so we can all finally appreciate the pivotal role he played in saving our country (God knows, none of us remembered), his heretofore lambasted action in pardoning President Nixon the burglar, is shown to be the critical move that kept this country from falling into civil war. At a time when everyone else in America wanted justice served, he stood alone before the blood thirsty mob at the guillotine and put justice in its proper place, not letting its indiscretions intrude on the men who've traditionally wielded power in our great country. Only Gerald Ford understood that the trauma of being so indiscriminately just and fair could bring this country down.

So what did he do? He took himself down. What a man!

Who knew?

I must apologize to the readers at this point, as the tears begin to cloud my vision and break my concentration. My guilt in not attending any of the seemingly innumerable services already held during the Gerald R. Ford Traveling Eulogy Show is now becoming overwhelming. Now that he is dead, we all know that any praise for this misunderstood man can only fall way short – but I can't go on.

See you in Grand Rapids.

Relevant Material: *In the essay "The News," I talk about a category of news coverage I dubbed "phony news," and explained the exaggerated importance the media gives to some events, as well as the excessive quantity of such news items given to the public by Big Media. The death of President Ford and its media coverage was a perfect example of "phony news." It is used as an almost pure form of propaganda. In this case, the idea is to give mythical status to all of our presidents.*

THE CHINESE ADVANTAGE

(4/10)

Amongst the ingrained traits of the neo-liberal global capitalism that has currently subdued the world, is its aggressive, competitive nature. It is a concept that naturally leads to confrontation and conflict. It is a Darwinian struggle for revenue where survival often boils down to rigging the system for the benefit of those at the top of its pyramid. But even if it worked as advertised, that is, competing business ventures finding success or failure through the quality of their product, its bellicose nature remains intact.

With the end of the ideological battles of the Cold War, the tealeaves left at the bottom of the cup did not purvey a clear message. This long running conflict, with its well defined battle lines, had become a habit that left an uncertain void with its passing. How would the tea leaves line up in a post-Cold War world?

We are now a generation into this Corrupt New World and the configuration for future confrontation is coming more into focus. The more visible manifestations of the status quo's fight with Islamic terrorism could easily be mistaken as an important aspect of this new world order. It is not. It has very little to do with the more all-encompassing global struggles of the current geo-economic system. It is no more than a sideshow brought about by the system's exaggerated need for energy. It is a minor outbreak of crabgrass on the lawn of business as usual.

The real battle seems to be shaping up between the long time champ, that being western capitalism led by the over confident, out of shape girth of the United States, and the hungry, up and coming young contender, The People's Republic of China. Whether or not a maturing European Community can now act independently of the United States remains to be seen, but it could be in a position to do so. It provides cheaper more effective medical services, better public education, it wastes almost nothing on useless military spending and, perhaps most of all, it is transitioning into a post-fossil fuel world with far more diligence than the decadent, Faroukian mentality of America's broken "democracy."

And that neatly leads us into the pulp of this essay, that being the advantage China might have in not having to stage the cumbersome burlesque called democracy, which seems to be limiting America's ability to react and evolve properly.

There is nobility in the idea of democracy that could be seen as worth the effort. I say this not just for romantic reasons, but because it could be considered the best path to human fruition. I'd sign on with those that say a truly functioning democracy will always be superior to any more authoritarian forms of government.

The problem is that American democracy is not functional. It only responds to one segment of the integral whole, that being large corporate interests. At the very least, we can comfortably say this one segment has an extremely undue amount of influence, one that does away with the true spirit of democracy. These interests, with the help of electoral mechanisms that make it easy for them to co-opt the system, have begun to monopolize political power. There may be a set back here and there, but the stubborn wallop of such huge sums of money eventually regains any ground lost. This might not be a permanent condition, but "change we can believe in" has always been a mirage-like concept just beyond the reach of the thirsty organism.

So the United States and China find themselves embroiled in the competitive conflict of global capitalism. There is much trade and cooperation, but in the end, as it always is, capitalism is a competition and each participant is trying to get the best of the other. You cannot enter this game without trying to win. It is the nature of the beast.

The question is, at this juncture in history, which competitor is more able to respond to the challenges of the moment – America's vaudevillian "democracy," or China's monolithic government?

The first thing we have to clear up is that gringo 2 party democracy has, approximately, the same amount of political parties as China's one party system. America's 2 parties are basically one party, that being the Business or Corporate Party. The ideological strains of thought operating within the confines of America's 2 parties are probably no more diverse than whatever strains of thought exist within China's ruling Communist Party. In fact, considering the changes that have taken place in China over the last ¼ century, there may even be more diverse debate within its singular political voice.

Being that the government of the United States, with its superficial stage production of 2-party democracy, has been almost thoroughly coerced by special interests that represent a small percentage of the nation's population, the author would like to raise a few questions:

1) Does the Chinese government respond more or less to the will and needs of its people than the American government?

2) Does the average citizen in America's democracy have more or less influence over its government than its Chinese counterpart?

For the average American, as steeped in its culture's propaganda as anyone else, such questions would seem ridiculous, if not blasphemous. How could anyone even suggest such things?

Someone's gotta do it.

I'm not here to provide the answers to these questions for the simple reason that I can't. But I am here to tell you that you can't either! These are debatable questions that should be on the table. With regard to question 1, there are indications that the Chinese government is more responsive. In the course of 25 to 30 years, it has taken a dogmatic, hard line communist regime into the brave new world of their form of capitalism. This could be considered revolutionary change, and it has been done without apocalyptic upheaval and only trace amounts of violence.

Meanwhile, (cue the Beatles) back in the U.S of A., its government has not taken action on a number of no-brainer issues since the times of Ronald Reagan, issues that are pivotal for the nation's healthy march into the future. First and foremost here is campaign finance reform. This is an obvious and easy to fix problem that still goes unattended to (see all essays with Campaign Reform in its title). Not only has this not been fixed, but recent actions by a conservative Supreme Court doing the bidding of their corporate masters, have set back a cause that has never begun, which almost goes against the laws of physics. The health care dilemma, in spite of the timid reform just passed by the Obama administration, is another buzzard circling over the agony of American progress. It is an ambiguous compromise still begging a better solution, and it too is a no-brainer. All one has to do is take a look around to see good models everywhere. And then there is the transition to a post-fossil fuel world, an area in which the United States has petulantly resisted getting out of the starting gate in a timely fashion. I shudder to think of the political Stalingrad awaiting any attempt at meaningful change on this issue. Other issues include breaking up media operations that have become oversized and monopolistic, a post-Cold War revamping of the country's military apparatus, on and on.

While China was making itself over in a way that could be likened to a leopard changing its spots, there has only been one meaningful change in post-Reagan America, that being a growing influence of corporate interests that could now be described as quasi-dictatorial. It can almost be said that these interests now regulate the government and not the old vice versa. While China continues to react dynamically to the world around it, post-Reagan America has stopped evolving. The only decisive actions it has taken have been expensive acts of warfare with little return.

With regard to question 2, that being the influence each country's average citizen has over its government, obviously, I know as much about how China's political mechanisms work as you do. What I do know is that America's local yokels have almost no influence over its government's decisions. The politicians they vote for are hand picked for them by the narrow corporate interests that run their parties. It is good theater, but it offers a very narrow range of ideology. It is the difference between an orange and a tangerine.

My guess is that Chinese politicians must curry favor with the Party in order to fulfill whatever ambitions they might have. It might not be that democratic, but it probably produces a competent kind of apparatchik, and the question still remains, is America's current form of "democracy" any more democratic? The Chinese politician doesn't have to suck up to large sums of private money. He doesn't have to look like Mitt Romney. He or she cannot profit from their sex appeal, like hot pants Sarah. Competence, as opposed to having "it," is most likely a larger element in the rise of a Chinese politician. He is part of a government that can govern, a government that can react, that can take important decisions.

Ronald Reagan ushered in an era of paralysis in American government. It is unduly influenced by corporate interests that frequently do not serve the interests of the broad cross section of the citizenry. It is neither democratic nor effective. I have no problem with corporations or Big Money being able to petition the government, like any other interest group. But we have reached a point where government must now petition Big Money in order to act. This drastically limits choices for solutions.

I do not favor Chinese style governance over true democracy. Open, democratic government is the most dynamic, creative, efficient way to serve the most people best. But if it is locked in a noose of narrow special interests, all these benefits of democracy are gelded. It gets passive, fat, lazy. It becomes less fertile, in bred, weaker. It mutates into something less productive spiritually. It begins to wallow in its own crap.

This is a big advantage for the Chinese in the game of global capitalism. They can react, evolve and blunder along objectively. They can redo mistakes. Meanwhile, the gringos mount their dog and pony show and peddle it as democracy. Nothing gets done, but hey, we're free, right?

Are we?

POLIOMYELITUS

(2/11)

Perhaps it is not obvious enough, so I will explain that the word forming the title of this essay pertains to the dreaded disease known more simply as "polio." Its place in history now seems almost "Babylonian" remote, but it was once one of the most feared diseases in the pantheon of human suffering, especially since its primary target was children who had still not had their chance at life. It severely affected motor skills and rendered beautiful young sprouts into withered, twisted weeds. It was a cause of widespread sorrow.

I can remember being on vacation in the Catskill Mountains when I was about 7 years old. Somewhere along the line, I developed a very stiff neck, which was not only extremely uncomfortable, but pretty much ruined the vacation atmosphere for everyone. The primary reason for this was the fear of it being polio, which was an immense boogieman in those days. No time was wasted in whisking me off to a doctor – don't worry, sighs of relief, a bullet dodged. But the "p" word ruled supreme. It was a parent's worst nightmare. When polio was finally suppressed, its conqueror, Dr. Jonas Salk, became a hero-celebrity of DiMaggio-like proportions. I'd guess most people still know the name.

This essay got its start when I received in the mail what we used to refer to as a "file card," more specifically, a 3 by 5 inch file card with the printed title "Poliomyelitis Vaccination Record" set forth at the top. My older sister must have been rummaging around in some ancient family documents when she found it and thought it might interest me.

It did.

That 3 by 5 file card was an informational record of a great scientific experiment I took part in when I was 9 years old. Dr. Salk had developed a polio vaccine that had shown promise wherever such scientific advancements show promise before being used by human beings. The last step was to actually try it on such creatures and it was decided to test it on New York City public school children, of which I was one. Before getting on to the most relevant philosophical element of this essay, I'd like to mention the following:

There was a time when the 3 by 5 file card was one of the most foundational elements of information storage in the world. Of course, today's digital world has rendered it as primitive as a caveman's club for weaponry, and yet, it played a pivotal role in one of the great scientific breakthroughs of modern times. It makes me wonder as to the spiritual worth of all this Twittering-Facebook neurosis and what it means for the clods feverishly pecking away on hand held devices that seem as addictive to them as a pack of cigarettes are to a nicotine addict. My guess is that these incredible communicative devices will create a new human being, but they will be fundamentally neutral in creating a more fulfilled human being.

In any event – the file card in question here had some lines and boxes printed on it which were filled in by hand by whoever was receiving the tax dollars to do so. The first thing I noticed was they had gotten my middle initial wrong, something that seemed to have little effect on the outcome of the great social undertaking. More important was a rectangular box of about 2 inches in length in the bottom left corner, divided into 3 smaller boxes. Each box showed the date, in ink, on which I was inoculated, the last in a series of 3 dated "11/22/55." In the lower right hand corner was something even more important: the words printed there said "Parental Request Received" with the date "3/29/55" hand written next to it.

But of course – the government didn't just go around using children in scientific experiments without telling anyone, at least not the children of free, white, adult Brooklyn Dodger fans deemed the respectable foundation for the American juggernaut in the world. By now, we all know the swastika-like story of the black sharecroppers used in venereal disease experiments without their knowledge. But that's another story –

So my parents, along with thousands of other parents, were asked by the government to loan them their children, like hey, don't worry, you'll get 'em back just fine. And this is where this essay begins to heat up some.

The question I asked myself as I looked at the date my parents agreed to all this, was whether there was any resistance or reluctance to the government's efforts? As I searched through my memory bank, I eventually concluded it had not been an issue. I have no memory of any angst-ridden debates in the household as to the propriety of all this, nor any remembrance of a more general debate in the community as a whole. In fact, I'd go even further by saying most people were glad to participate, were happy to be part of such an important socio-scientific attempt to improve the human condition, were proud to display the solidarity of their good citizenship in conjunction with their neighbors. Their country, through its governmental organism, was asking for their help and they trusted it. Sure, go ahead, it's our civic duty. Why wouldn't we accept?

This feeling managed to seep into our little kids' minds as well. As I remember, the experiment was administered in the public schools (my file card referenced PS 205, in Queens). Even though no kid relishes the idea of getting stuck with a needle, my participation was angst free. This is not to say I marched down to the school nurse with a well defined sense of duty or purpose, but in some barely conscious, kids' kind of way, we understood we were doing something good, and not just for ourselves, but for everyone.

And this is where the ripest pulp of this essay began to mature. As I pondered my parents' permission, I had to ask myself if such a great, "socialistic," governmental undertaking could happen in today's America. Could we pull together in such a way, under the umbrella of the government's stewardship, to accomplish such a positive goal?

After due reflection, I had to sadly conclude that such a possibility seemed somewhat remote. The turning point, in this man's opinion, began with the rise of 2 men in the United States whose names I've mentioned together before in these pages: Ronald Reagan and Rupert Murdoch. Their importance in American socio-political relevance began at about the same time. Reagan was the first politician to make the anti-government rhetoric popular. His famous statement, "the government is the problem, not the solution," has become Gospel for the special interests that want less and less supervision. With a huge media conglomerate like Murdoch's constantly evangelizing this attitude, the anti-government rhetoric has sunk deep roots in the American psyche. The idea of a Social Contract administered for the common good by the people's government, outside of a "market" framework, has been riddled with right wing machine gun fire led by Murdoch's Fox News. And, in a circular way, it becomes self-prophetic. Here's how:

We have an electoral process that is so expensive to compete in only those with special interest bankrolls (oil companies, drug companies, insurance companies, other varied and assorted Wall St. vultures) can get elected. This creates a government that does not want to govern, to supervise, to referee, because our elected officials work for special interests that want the government off their backs. The result of this is **BAD GOVERNMENT!** When things go bad, as they have since the appearance of the dynamic duo mentioned above (I defy anyone to claim things are better now than before our now deified presidential clod and the ruthless media magnate began working their spell on America), the only place the voter can put the blame is with this bad government. This further encourages the "government is the problem" rhetoric.

For too long now, Americans have been confusing bad government with the idea that government is the problem. Our idea of good citizenship is being perverted. The empathy necessary to work for the common good through a Social Contract we've all created as working pieces in the grand scheme of our nation, is disappearing. The average American has been distilled down into little more than an individual island competing against all the other individuals for the spoils of the consumer society. Some win, some lose, some draw – and who really cares beyond that?

The ultimate perversion of this "every man for himself" attitude is reflected in the way the nation fights its grimy little imperial wars. The "volunteer army" (for more, see essay The Volunteer Army) is not a citizen's army. It is not a patriot army. It is not a Social Contract army defending the country as part of one's civic duty.

No!

It is a mercenary army manned by people who, for diverse reasons having less to do with patriotism or duty and more to do with their options in life, have been bribed by the rest of us who have better things to do. For the last decade or so, we've been recycling the same microscopic portion of our population through war zones while the rest of us watch football games rife with praise and appreciation for their efforts, deaths and mutilations. What, me worry?

This is the attitude America now lives in. It is an attitude that may have sabotaged the great polio vaccine experiment I was proud to have been a part of.

Post Data: In an amazing display of coincidence, while writing this essay the horrifying shootings in Tucson, Arizona took place, killing 6, including a 9 year old girl and a Federal Judge, wounding many, and leaving a United States Congresswoman in a vegetable state. Although it is dangerous to attribute this to anything more than the actions of a deranged lunatic, the perpetrator's lunacy does seem to be fueled to some extent by this anti-government, libertarian strain of thought that has grown exponentially in post Reagan-Murdoch America.

Relevant Material: I quote from a novel called "The Desert" (El Desierto) by a Chilean-German writer named Carlos Franz. The character named Laura was a young judge in the Allende government in Chile when the military coup that ousted him occurred. Franz's novel is an ode to what happened and where Chile went from there. He writes, "If the fate of Laura's era had been tragic, if her generation had been the last one to grow up with ideals, ideals they had the chance to see demolished and refuted along with their youth, the fate of her daughter and those of her age, and those that would come after, were worse than tragic, it was a farce. When the same tragedies repeat themselves, they do it as farces – "

THE END OF DEMOCRACY REVISITED

(12/11)

It's been 22 months since I wrote my first essay on perhaps the greatest judicial error since the days of slavery, that being the now infamous "Citizens United" case (see essay, "2010: The End of Democracy"). This is the case where the United States Supreme Court, in a 5 to 4 decision, ruled that any laws attempting to limit the amount of money any person or corporation can contribute to a political candidate is unconstitutional. The decision is based upon the premise that corporate money contributed to a candidate is akin to the free speech guaranteed in the Constitution. In a political system that is failing due to the dominance of moneyed interests, this is something like trying to cure lung cancer by smoking cigarettes.

As the months have gone by and the political punditry class of American media continues to wrestle with the ramifications of this decision, I find something terribly lacking in their analysis, especially amongst those who are justifiably outraged by this ruling. They are not getting to the pith of the matter, to the reason why this decision is such a threat to the democracy so beautifully constructed in the Constitution. Sure, we get it; these huge sums of undeclared political contributions are co-opting the electoral process. True, this is bad enough, but it is not the worst aspect of Citizens United.

What makes this ruling so prejudicial to our whole idea of democratic governance is the following: the conservative judges responsible for this fiasco are acting in a political way, not a judicial way. This is a frontal attack on the checks and balances envisioned in the 3 branches of government, a system meant to diffuse the concentration of power in too few people. I find very little discussion of this by our most renowned political pundits.

Someone's gotta do it.

I will now prove this to you, using a set of circumstances our political pundits are failing either to enunciate clearly or put forth at all, something I touched upon in the "End of Democracy" essay. Given the skeletal, or even inexistent treatment of the subject, I feel the need to further expound upon these neglected circumstances. By so doing, the spectacular hypocrisy of these conservative judges will become evident, a hypocrisy that can only lead one to believe they are acting more like politicians than judges.

The first thing that must be established here is that these conservative judges refer to themselves as "strict constructionists" of the Constitution. It is relevant to note this label is not hung on them by others, but self-proclaimed loudly. This means, according to **THEM**, that they do not like anyone taking liberties with the exact wording of the document, that no one should read things into the Constitution that are not exactly set forth therein.

Fine. Let's apply these principles to an actual Supreme Court ruling.

Roe v. Wade, like Citizens United, is a landmark decision in American jurisprudence. It granted women their constitutional right to terminate a pregnancy – or, more specifically, it ruled unconstitutional any law meant to take this right away. Before getting into the reasons used to come to this decision, it must be emphasized that a judge hearing this case was not ruling on whether or not an abortion is a good or bad thing, a moral or immoral thing, or anything else having to do with how one might feel about such an action. The judge's personal feelings should not enter into the decision. The only thing being decided in Roe v. Wade is if a law denying a woman's right to control her own bodily functions is permissible under the Constitution.

But let's also be realistic. Judges are human beings, which means they have concepts of right and wrong, good and evil, and, like the rest of us, a worldview in general. If you are a good judge, you should fight these tendencies when trying to apply the law objectively, even if you do not like the law. But, as we've said, humans will be humans.

I am a person who believes sincerely in a woman's right to choose. If I had sat on the court that heard Roe v. Wade, I'm sure I'd have looked for something in the Constitution to justify that stance. However, even if I did not consider myself a "strict constructionist" in the conservative sense, I'd certainly limit my roaming to something very plausible in making the case for a woman's right to choose. If I could not find that plausible justification in the document, I would go against my own personal feelings on abortion and rule only within the meaning of the Constitution. This is how any judge should go about their business.

Fortunately, for a pro-choice person, that plausible connection could be found in the form of the "right to privacy" even though the Constitution does not specifically speak of such a right. The vehicle used to reach this conclusion was the 9th amendment, which says that any other rights not clearly enunciated in the Constitution will not be denied simply for that reason. The Supreme Court justices that gave the pro-choice stance its victory in Roe v. Wade, felt a woman's constitutionally guaranteed "right to privacy" was being denied her if she could not terminate a pregnancy. Be one pro-choice or pro-life, it is hard to deny there is some nexus between the idea of privacy and a woman's ability to control her own bodily functions (I repeat that phrase because it seems to get to the crux of the matter). Indeed, any society that believes in private property must, it seems, also have deeply ingrained feelings for the idea of privacy – and what could be more private than one's own control of your body?

But for the conservative judges, the self proclaimed "strict constructionists" (who, by the way, are all pro-life), this "right to privacy" linked to a woman's right to choose is an unforgivable stretching of the Constitution's meaning. It is reading something into it that is just not there. They dissent!

Fine. Even if I feel the ruling in Roe v. Wade is a correct one in a purely constitutional sense, the "strict constructionists" have their point of view and if they stay consistent, I can respect that.

They've lost my respect.

Fast-forward to 2010 and the Citizens United case. The problem of money in our political system is obvious. Quite logically, in an attempt to have a democracy with some resemblance to the word, legislative bodies are propagating laws meant to limit campaign contributions, especially from corporations, where the real money is. These laws are soon challenged as an impediment to the "free speech" guaranteed us all in the Constitution (I know, it's hard not to laugh – or cry). Citizens United will decide this issue.

Unlike the days of Roe v. Wade, the conservative "strict constructionists" now have a majority on the court. They have all been nominated by conservative Republican presidents. Although, theoretically, this should not influence their decisions, they are, if not card carrying but in their hearts, Republicans. Republicans like money in politics, even more than the Democrats. Regardless of your cynicism with regard to both Parties being involved in this money game, the truth is this: Republicans still work for the wealthiest elements of our society; Republicans find easier access to the largest sums of money than Democrats do, especially at electoral levels below that of the president; Republicans want unbridled access to this money, something that, in the long run, would prejudice their opposition.

It must be reiterated that what is being decided in Citizens United is not whether you like or dislike money in politics. For a Supreme Court justice, that should not be the issue. The only thing a judge should be thinking about is if a law restricting money in politics is permissible under the Constitution.

So here we go. When the dust has settled the conservative "strict constructionists" give victory to the moneyed interests by ruling all these laws limiting campaign contributions are unconstitutional. Why? Because money is a form of speech.

What?!!!

Not only that, but corporations, through their money, have this right to free speech.

What?!!!!!

Here they are, these self proclaimed "strict constructionists," the same guys who can't find a close enough connection between the "right to privacy" logically arrived to in the Constitution and a woman's right to choose, now creating this tortured, Byzantine metaphor which makes corporations giving campaign dollars in the millions a form of free speech!

Where does it say anything resembling that in the Constitution?

Case closed. Such hypocrisy can only lead to one conclusion: these conservative judges are <u>politicians</u> not jurists. They are acting politically not judicially. They are "strict constructionists" only when it suits their political agenda. This is a serious breach of protocol, one that destroys the whole concept of the democracy so elegantly laid out by The Founders.

There are many good people in our media establishment protesting strenuously against Citizens United and its adverse effects on American democracy. They have even set in motion the embryonic first steps towards a constitutional amendment allowing restrictions of money in politics. I'm not against such efforts, but it puts focus in the wrong direction. It is a surrender to flagrant judicial malfeasance. Our Constitution can clearly accommodate restrictions of money in our political process, but a few conservative politicians masquerading as judges have blown up the system. Their hypocrisy is obvious. They've been caught red handed. Anyone with a camera or microphone in front of them; anyone with a political column in any publication or blog, should be hitting hard on this. If these conservative judges are going to act like politicians, they should be treated like politicians. A constitutional amendment that is really not necessary would set a bad precedent. It would let the villains off. It would legitimize politics in the judicial branch. It would mean anytime a politician masquerading as a judge makes a ridiculous, politically motivated decision, we'd have to amend the Constitution.

That is unacceptable.

Post Script: Quite coincidentally, one of the most pompous fools in American political history, Newt Gingrich, recently suggested that judges making silly or politically motivated decisions should be called before congress to explain themselves, or even be arrested! This is another way of destroying the wisdom of our Constitution because it would make judges dependent on the approval of politicians to survive. Judges must be able to act independently of such pressures if their role in our society is to be fulfilled. What I am suggesting is media sources calling them out stridently for blatant transgressions of their judicial role. They should at least be judged in the court of public opinion for these politically inspired decisions and it is media's role to make these things understandable to the average citizen.

It is ironic that clowns like Newt Gingrich and his conservative bedfellows have been the most vociferous policemen in pursuit of "activist" judges who bend the law for their own political purposes. And yet, the Citizens United case is the strongest case for such criticism in my lifetime. If Newt was not the mega hypocrite he's always been, he should be calling for the arrest of justices Scalia, Thomas, Roberts, et al.

THE ELECTION OF 2012

(11/12)

It has almost become a cliché to say the presidential election of the moment is the "most important election of our times" or something to that effect. If I were to really proclaim a presidential election just that, it might be the 1932 election of Franklin Delano Roosevelt, which changed the way we do capitalism forever. But the well armed forces of quasi-oligarchic mega-wealth have never stopped trying to turn the clock back to those good old days of pre-Delano depression economies. Their tireless efforts had just about triumphed when the crash of 2008 blew up the game. This should have been a knockout blow to the "supply side" market mavens, but their mechanisms of propaganda have been so well developed in the last ¼ century it enabled them to strategically retreat before the inevitable Obama victory in 2008 in able to go on fighting (kind of like a political Dunkerque).

The plan was to sabotage Obama's presidency by not allowing him to repair the economy, a tactic that could have been defeated in the first 2 years of Obama's mandate if he had shown more leadership (see essays "Scary Economic Stuff" and "Barak Obama: Health Care We Didn't Get"). The Republican Party, doing the bidding of their plutocratic sources of funding, purposely kept the American people in 4 more years of economic suffering so they could eventually define it as the failure of Barak Obama.

It almost worked. Only the combination of sub-standard presidential material in the Republican Party and the personal qualities of Barak Obama kept it from happening.

With regard to importance, I'd call the election of 2012 the runner up to that of 1932. In many ways the same battle lines had been drawn. Should we go back to a purely Darwinian form of pre-Social Contract "savage capitalism"? Should the government forgo its role as the referee who makes the market behave? Should the private sector be free to do whatever it wants? Should we rely solely upon the market to naturally regulate itself? The fact that we were re-fighting these battles is a testament to the conservative media's huge sound machine and the force of its propaganda mechanisms.

The election of 2012 was one in which both sides were risking it all. The loser would be, if not dead, severely moribund in the foreseeable future. Waterloo, Gettysburg, Stalingrad, the course of history was about to change.

Let's start with the Democrats.

Perhaps the strongest position the Democrats could dig in with was that the economic suffering of the American people was the direct result of neo-con Republican ideology. Taxes on the super rich, the so called "job creators," were the lowest in memory, the government's regulatory apparatus had become almost ceremonial and the private sector was free of all defenders as it ran to pay dirt –

– until the predictable crash such policies always lead to arrived in 2008.

If we leave aside the radical social conservatism that has infested the Republican Party – we will get back to it – what is the core of Republicanism? It is referred to in a number of ways: neo-liberal capitalism, supply side economics, the University of Chicago or Friedman school of economics, trickle down theory, etc. In its most distilled form, it postulates a market place let to naturally regulate itself, a market place free of government supervision, a market place that should not have to surrender almost any of its earnings to a public sector that should almost be done away with. This is an "apparatchik-like" way to say almost no taxation, especially on the upper spheres of wealth.

Certainly, if we go back to the 1950's and such, when this economic idea was finding its footing (before the Great Depression it existed simply by accident), there were many "true believers" and some are still around today – David Frum? Paul Ryan? George Will? But history has shown there is little empirical evidence to suggest this actually benefits the greater good, in fact, just the opposite seems more empirically true. If "supply side" and such is still a vibrant player in economic debate, it is only because it benefits the wealthy and powerful, which is the same reason it found acceptance to begin with. It is an ideology used as a smoke screen for personal interests. The Bushes, Romneys, Koch brothers and such are "Freidmanites" only in the sense that it works for them.

When Obama came to power in 2008, the "supply side" idea was in tatters. Its wounds were festering and there was nowhere to hide it. In spite of the fact that he inherited a critically ill patient made sick by just what his opponents had prescribed, he did a mediocre job of defending a strong ideological position. He tried to do the right thing – stimulus, job acts, Keynesian governmental action in general – but he let a minority Republican presence push him around. By 2010, he had no numerical ability to stop the Republican saboteurs, who would try to pin the lackluster recovery on him. But –

– the Republicans offered absolutely no new ideas in how to fix the damage they had done – none, zero, nada, zilch, kaput, a goose egg. It is one thing to criticize, to denigrate, to rile against something, and quite another to offer solutions – and offering the same solutions that led to the wreckage was still not an advantageous position. Couple this with a Mitt Romney already seriously damaged by the primary process; a Mitt Romney seriously flawed by his flip-flopping attempts to please the daffy wing of his party; a Mitt Romney, stiff, uncomfortable, almost paranoiac with supporters who were hating Obama much more than loving him –

Regardless of the prevailing economic mediocrity, if the Democrats could not win in this environment it would be a devastating blow. It would mean the right wing sound machine was capable of defending an indefensible position. It may have meant the end of the liberal or progressive idea as we know it.

It would be what many pundits were beginning to refer to as a "post-truth world."

As for the Republicans, I'd like to start with 2 quotes from previous essays, quotes that proved very prophetic. In the essay "Rush Limbaugh or American Fascism," written in 2009, I said, "These social conservatives have become *too big to fail.* Like the Nazis of old, they are fanatic in their beliefs and in no mood for compromise. They've been the Republican Party's most loyal stockholders and now they want to own it." Later on, in May of 2012, I wrote the following in the essay "The Strategy of Water" with regard to the social conservatives influence in the Republican Party: "– it has made the Party accept social positions beyond the realm of reason for most Americans. This Republican-Tea Party alliance has created a neo-conservative party now flirting with the word *radical.* There will be dues to pay somewhere down the line."

The election of 2012 was the culmination of this struggle within the Republican Party. I say "struggle" because this coalition of social conservatives and the traditional core of generational Republicans trying to protect their economic interests, is an unnatural mutant. It is like a bad marriage whose initial fascination has worn off leaving the 2 sides with nothing in common. Now that the social conservatives have mustered enough strength within the Party to actually influence its actions – up until now, the traditional Republicans paid lip service but little more – the bickering (war?) has begun.

Mitt Romney, in this writer's opinion, is a very mediocre man, but he is not an intellectual troglodyte. Being the mediocre person he is, in order to capture the Republican Party's nomination, he accepted his own self flagellation in trying to placate the social conservatives. He had to publicly accept zygotes as human beings, belittle science, show scorn for Darwin, cringe at the thought of birth control, attack such "monstrous" organizations as Planned Parenthood, denigrate such "villainous" creatures as school teachers, attack such dastardly mind polluters as Public Broadcasting, and generally act in the cretinous way his Party has evolved into. He has had to bob and weave his way through social conservative minefields of almost pre-historic thought. It made him look like the mediocre man he is.

Mitt Romney's experience is a microcosm of the whole Republican Party at the moment. Its defeat in 2012 can be attributed to many factors, but the strength of the social conservatives could be considered, at the very least, the tipping point of its debacle. The traditional wing of the Party could no longer keep a lid on the incendiary rhetoric of the social conservatives and America rejected it.

This marriage between the social conservatives and the "traditionalists" has broken up. In the end, it had to be so because one side (the traditionalists) was using the other. It was not true love. It was an act, a ploy, and the divorce will not be amicable. The fight for the failed marriage's assets will now begin. In the foreseeable future, I see no good roads for the Party to go down. People like Paul Ryan are not going away and if his wing takes over, that is, it is decided they lost because they did not present an authentic enough brand of conservatism, they continue to lose almost everywhere but their small congressional fiefdoms. If the Party tries to wean itself of the social issues ball and chain and tries to win solely on its economic policies (as well as its hawkish foreign policy), it alienates a large block of its most enthusiastic voters.

The Republican Party could find itself wandering in the wilderness for quite some time.

EGYPT, 2013

(8/13). This is the first of 2 related essays, the second being "American Exceptionalism."

In much the same way a carelessly disposed cigarette can set off a fire that destroys 100's of square miles of tinder dry forest, the so called "Arab Spring" has set much of the Middle East ablaze. One looking at a forest in such a perilous state of thirst hardly notices any abnormality. It is only after the seemingly insignificant spark ignites it that we realize just how serious the situation was.

That seemingly insignificant spark occurred in one of the world's more anonymous countries, little Tunisia. It set off a huge conflagration that eventually engulfed Bahrain, Yemen, Libya, Syria, and the Big Kahuna of all Arab states, Egypt. It is a blaze that has still not been contained, with Syria engaged in a full-fledged civil war and Egypt on the brink of one. All this without even mentioning the combustible conditions that still exist in any Arab country not named here, including the west's most important client state in the region, the petro-dollar monster known as Saudi Arabia. No smoking, no camp fires, this forest is ready to ignite with one false move.

Egypt is a country of almost 100 million people with a strategic canal running through it. Any imperial power worth its weight in world influence cannot ignore this place. When the Egyptian military, the traditional broker for American interests in the country, overthrew the democratically elected government which emerged in the wake of the Arab Spring, it put the United States in an awkward position. On the one hand, the removal of a government not to its liking; of a government too Islamic for its taste; of a government not sympathetic to or controlled by American interests, had to put a wry smile of satisfaction on the face of American foreign policy (at this point, who knows how much of an active role the U.S. played in the "coup" it refuses to call such?). On the other hand, it once again exposes what can only be called the long running, traditional hypocrisy of America's foreign policy rhetoric, with its romantic evocations of democracy, liberty, freedom, cue the marching band, sound the trumpets – but remember, someone we like has to win, or it is not a democracy.

When I originally began postulating the things I might say in this essay, I vaguely remembered a passage I'd underlined in a novel by the Mexican master, Carlos Fuentes (Mexico has produced 2 of the 20th century's greatest intellects in Fuentes and the poet-philosopher, Octavio Paz). Thankfully, I still had the book amidst the modest paperback library with which I line the walls of my modest dwelling place. It is a novel named "*Diana o la cazadora solitaria*" (Diana or the lonely hunter) published in 1994. If, I thought, the passage in question is relevant, I'd use it as an addendum to the essay, something I occasionally do under the title "Relevant Material."

When I reread the passage I had to change my plans. It so perfectly captured the essence of what I was rolling around in my mind, I decided to quote it in the text of this essay. In the following essay, "American Exceptionalism," I will translate the 2 pages leading up to this passage in order to provide a fuller context for the more curious reader.

The passage in question, in English, goes like this: *"The United States defines its foreign policy as a totally selfless exercise, as almost an act of philanthropy. Since this has never been the case for any great power, including the United States, nobody believes it, but the self-delusions of the American people drive everyone crazy. Everyone knows what kinds of interests are in play, but the Americans are not allowed to admit it. What they are doing, selflessly, of course, is spreading liberty, democracy, is saving everyone else from themselves."*

It makes perfect sense that a person from Latin America would understand the Gringo pathos in its most minute derivations. For more than a century, the symptoms of this sickness lodged themselves in the body of a whole hemisphere. This is where the United States most perfected its imperial hypocrisy. This is where the Americans composed their song of liberty, freedom and democracy while materially supporting some of the most vulgar, despotic regimes in history. There is hardly a place anywhere south of the Rio Grande that has not felt the wrath of the "Yanqui" colossus when attempting to extricate itself from the yolk of such colonialism. Who better than Carlos Fuentes, one of Latin America's greatest thinkers, to understand and transmit the imperial hypocrisy of the United States of America?

Fuentes corroborates the core of what I want to express in this essay, to wit: the United States is no better or worse than any great imperial power that preceded it, but it is the only one that has ever tried to rationalize or sanitize its self serving actions with the claim it is doing it for the benefit of everyone else.

That is pukeable.

And these same dynamics are still in play in the Middle East, where the hypocrisy of America's rhetoric juxtaposed against its actions has gotten it into an untenable situation.

It is ironic that Latin America now finds itself somewhat free of the American colonial noose due to its over-extension into a part of the world the United States now feels is more essential to its self interest. For the last half century or so, the world's only "Stupid Power" has used the exact same playbook in the Arab world as it did in Latin America. There is much talk of democracy and freedom but the true goal is to propagate client states that follow the rules of the American game. The only difference, in the American mind set, between the Mubarak regime in Egypt and the Khadafy regime in Libya or the Assad regime in Syria was that the former was "our" dictator while the latter 2 were not. People tend to forget that tyrants like Saddam Hussein and Manuel Noriega in Panama, were "our" dictators at one time. It was not their undemocratic governance that brought the American hammer down on them, but rather, their decision to not play ball with Uncle Sam anymore.

But the Middle East is a much more complicated and difficult place to manage for the Americans. The culture and the dynamics of how it works is far less understood than that of Latin America and the great snake oil salesman of democracy seems to lack the intellect to try and understand it.

Regardless of whatever governments in the region are controlled by American and western interests, this does not change the fact that the rank and file Arab does not, to put it mildly, sympathize with the Americans. They've seen millions of bombs dropped on their brethren in wars manufactured by the American empire worried for its oil supply. The continued one-sided sponsorship of the Jewish state in Palestine is a spine that still causes great pain and bleeding in the body of the Arab world. As a result –

When that careless campfire cinder in Tunisia set the whole Arab forest ablaze (the Tunisian dictator was "our" dictator), there was little the Americans could do to control it. All they could do was sit back and make propaganda glorifying the Arab Spring and its noble struggle for democracy and freedom, while cursing it under its breath for the loss of control and uncertainty it meant. The uprising in Egypt against Mubarak, given the usual Gringo rhetoric about the freedom to pursue the happiness of a new car, was something it could not oppose – at least in the moment. It would try everything in its power to influence the outcome, but with the good old democracy foot in its mouth –

It's a fine mess you've gotten us into, Ollie.

The problem the United States faces in this context is the following: if anything close to a democracy is put in play in the Middle East, it is highly unlikely anyone representing American interests will win. And that is exactly what happened in Egypt.

The Egyptian military's overthrow of the duly elected Morsi-Moslem Brotherhood regime leaves nothing but a big fat question mark on the future. In the short run, perhaps American interests are served, but such a myopic approach to foreign policy does little more than lead to the next crisis. In an admittedly more utopian vein, if America stood true to its Statue of Liberty rhetoric, and encouraged those upset with the Morsi regime to better organize in order to defeat it in the next elections, the chance of a fledgling democracy beginning to root itself in Arab soil might have a chance. If the Morsi regime truly overstepped its legal mandate – something that does not seem to be the case – and began eradicating the democracy that elected it, then a popular uprising against it, even led by the military, could be supported by the United States without contradicting its principles.

If the United States is to champion democracy in the world, it must respect and deal with any government elected fairly, unless it adheres to policies beyond the acceptance of world consensus (killing Jews, mutilating women, etc.), or tries to "totalitarianize" the democracy that put it in power, neither of which seems to be the case in today's Egypt. By being the usual imperial hypocrites it always has been, the United States has managed little more than to splatter a bit more egg on its face.

For a better understanding of Carlos Fuentes' view of American culture and how it affects its foreign policy, a view that is still relevant today, see next essay, "American Exceptionalism."

SHUT DOWNS,
DEBT CEILINGS, ETC.

(10/13)

I can't listen to it anymore; government shut downs, debt ceilings, the threat of this or that. Anyone with even a superficial knowledge of my thinking knows I consider the Republicans the villains here, and in the least uncertain terms. But, ironically, it is the less than adequate defense of their position by the Democrats that has led to this essay. Although everything I am about to say has already been said in this clamorous debate, I still find myself pleading with the progressive spokespeople to be more effective with their arguments, to be more efficient, to have the message more honed and ready for battle. While watching all this on TV, I sometimes feel like that eager rookie on the end of the bench.

"C'mon coach, I'm better than these guys."

As a result, I will now pretend to have my own political talk show on the PCM Network (Post Consumer Man Network).

Post Consumer Man - Good evening ladies and gentlemen, and welcome to the PCM Network's presentation of Politics and Nausea. If politics make you sick, this is the show for you. My guest this evening is Republican Congressman Travis Hayseed from North

Carolina, who represents a district including parts of Tobacco, Catfish, Stonewall Jackson, Trinity and Yeehaw counties in Congress. Welcome to the show Representative Hayseed.

Representative Hayseed – Thanks for having me, it's a pleasure to be here.

PCM – Congressman, how is it that your district includes so many counties?

Rep H – (He shrugs) that's how they drew it up.

PCM – In preparing for this show, I saw that it has a peculiar shape, like a drop of paint splattering on the floor.

Rep H – (He shrugs again) –

PCM – You generally win your elections by a wide margin, correct?

Rep H – (Smiling) I'm a good congressman.

PCM – I also found that the few Democrats who go to Congress from your state generally win by large margins as well.

Rep H – So?

PCM – Well, in the last congressional election, Democrats got more votes statewide than Republicans, but there are 9 Republicans and only 4 Democrats from North Carolina in Congress. How do you explain that?

Rep H – My job is to represent my district and that is what I do.

There is a loud silence. PCM begins to shuffle his notes. He clears his throat and continues.

PCM – Right. We are here to talk about your Party's attempts to shut down the government and not raise the debt ceiling. Representative Hayseed, these are super drastic things to do just because you do not like the

Affordable Care Act, which is not a Bill in Congress, but a duly constituted **Law** of the land.

Rep H – We don't see it like that. This Law is such an abomination –

PCM – Excuse me, excuse me, Congressman, but I must interrupt. How can you call it an abomination when it is just entering its infant stages? That is something like putting a month old baby in jail because he looks like a crook.

Rep H – Obamacare is an aberration and the American people agree with me.

PCM – Oh, I see, you've gotten the memo. Just keep saying it and it will become the truth –

Rep H – It is the truth.

PCM – No sir, the American people have not rejected the ACA. They are confused about it, but their actions more than suggest they are willing to give it a chance.

Rep H – That is not what my constituents tell me.

PCM – Your constituents make up an infinitesimal part of the United States. They have a right to their opinions and a right to impose them if they control the governing apparatus of the country sufficiently, something they do not at this moment.

Rep H – I beg your pardon, but enough people like them now control the House of Representatives.

PCM – I beg your pardon, but the ACA was passed in that very same chamber. The people who supported it **won an election**. Through the use of a democratic process, they controlled enough of the government to make it a law, something your Party has not been able to do in trying to repeal it. Your attempts to sabotage it with debt ceilings and shut downs are akin to a banana republic coup.

Rep H – The stakes here are way too high to not use whatever means necessary to stop it. Obamacare is so onerous, so detrimental to our nation's future – I cannot sit back and do nothing, and the American people support me.

PCM leans back and takes a deep breath. He rubs his eyes, blinks and goes on.

PCM – I repeat, as for the onerous nature of the ACA, you have no empirical evidence to back that up. You are judging the team before Opening Day arrives.

Rep H – Sometimes you know a team is bad before the season starts, and the polls I've seen back me up.

PCM – But every team is given the chance to prove itself and the objective prognostications for the ACA are not that bad to begin with. As for the polls you've seen, there is only one poll that counts and it is the biggest, most all encompassing poll of all, that being a presidential election. That seems to be the one poll you ignore. In 2012 your Party made repeal of the ACA one of the focal points of its campaign. The issue was mega-debated and litigated – and you lost!! You lost the presidency, you lost seats in the Senate, and you lost seats in the House. In fact, if not for the shape of districts like yours, you'd probably be the minority in the House as well. I remind you, more people voted for Democrats than Republicans in nation wide House races, and by a not insignificant number. So don't come to me with that American people stuff.

Rep H – The districts are what they are precisely because we **won** elections.

PCM – And in winning those local elections your only strategy for the American people, other than to return to a status quo that caused the greatest financial calamity since 1929 and a health care system that spends far more and gets far less than other proven models, is to gerrymander districts and suppress voter participation. You've offered nothing more than that – and you brag about it!

Rep H – Look, you can spin it however you want, but I cannot allow Obamacare to destroy this country.

Once again, there is a gaping silence as both men regather themselves. PCM grabs a pitcher of water from the coffee table separating the 2 men. He pours a glass and offers it to his guest, who accepts and takes a refreshing swallow as PCM pours himself a glass. When he is through sipping it, he clears his throat and renews the debate.

PCM – Congressman, being that the ACA is just entering the starting gate, we have to assume your pessimism is a prediction, correct?

Rep H – (He shrugs and ambiguously nods) –

PCM – Considering the track record of your Party over the last 10 years or so, that is, its failure to envision the disasters in Iraq and Afghanistan –

Rep H – Hold it! I am a Tea Party congressman. We do not favor such actions.

PCM – Commendable, but the excessive deregulatory policies your group would be even more extreme with caused the greatest financial debacle since the Great Depression. Why couldn't you predict that?

Rep H – That's your interpretation, and what's that have to do with Obamacare?

PCM – Well, if you are going to make these apocalyptic predictions, you don't seem to be a very good handicapper. Why should we believe your predictions for the ACA without at least trying it?

Rep H – (While pouring himself another glass of water) Well – I must vote my feelings. (He takes a swallow) It will cause job loss, higher premiums –

PCM – Yeah, yeah, and a national outbreak of herpes too. Look, Congressman, let's just hypothetically say you are right –

Rep H – It's not hypothetical.

PCM – Suit yourself. So here we are, the ACA stinks, just like you say. I remind you, Representative Hayseed, we are a democracy that has a nation wide election every 2 years. If it turns out to be as bad as you predict, you should be able to win the next election easily, as well as the presidential election in 2016. If you want to undo the policies of the Obama administration, that is the proper way to do it – win an election!

Rep H – We cannot wait that long –

PCM – A year? You're saying the United States cannot survive a year of the ACA? We've survived a great civil war, the Great Depression, the Dust Bowl, Vietnam, the Soviet Union and more, but one year of the ACA will bring us down?

Rep H – Better safe than sorry.

PCM – I'll have to let that be the last word. Representative Hayseed, thanks so very much for being here (he reaches across the table and shakes his hand).

Rep H – The pleasure was all mine.

PCM – After this short commercial break, I'll be back with my final comments.

PCM – Welcome back. In finishing tonight, I will resort to a bit of theater. (He turns his back to the camera) When I turn around I want you to think of me as President Obama addressing the nation in response to the government shut down and the debt ceiling issue. (He turns around)

Good evening. We are currently embroiled in a governing crisis that is not only totally unnecessary, but an affront to the democracy we proudly live in. In 2008 my Party won an election that gave us control of the Presidency, the Senate, and the House of Representatives. As a result, we were able to pass a law, the Affordable Care Act. For something like 4 years now, the Republican opposition has ridiculed it, defamed it, lied about it, and let loose everything in their arsenal in an all out carpet bombing to convince the American people to reject it. We've been through 2 election cycles since it became the law of the land and, in spite of their crusade to destroy it, they have still not been able to muster the electoral strength necessary to achieve their goals. In 2012, they made repeal of the Affordable Care Act an essential element of their campaign – and they lost seats in both chambers of Congress, as well as the Presidency. If the American people are so against the ACA, as the Republicans say, that seems a peculiar way to manifest it. As a result, in lieu of winning elections, the Republicans have decided to make an end run around our democracy with tactics that can only be considered cynical and even unpatriotic. But I warn them – your end run has run out of bounds. If you want to get back on the field and in the game, you must honorably compete for the votes of the American people. If you don't like my policies or anyone else's, **win an election**. That is how a democracy works. Thank you for your attention and have a good evening.

And that wraps up this edition of "Politics and Nausea."

PART III

PROPAGANDA, MEDIA, HOW THEY GET US TO BELIEVE SUCH CRAP

THE DEMORALIZED ZONE (DMZ)

(This essay was written in the early 90's)

I was recently standing in line at a food store chatting with a friend when a lovely young woman, accompanied by her equally attractive younger sister, burst into our male consciousness. Being that the older sister knew my friend, she came over and introduced her sibling, such younger version being blond, pert, intelligent, and no less than a student at Harvard University (whatever happened to Smith ... or was it Wellesley?). She was what my generation of collegians used to refer to as "cute," meaning we'd cross the Sahara Desert in a sand storm with only a bag of salted peanuts for the chance to get into her pants. In fact, she was cute enough to fall catatonically in love with in the hope of living happily ever after. As the rude experience of life has shown me, the catatonic love is much easier than the "happily ever after."

So there I was, thirty years removed from that naive campus mentality, an experienced man who'd seen and done it all, thinking I'd cross the Sahara Desert in a sand storm ... when my friend asked her what she was majoring in.

"Public Relations" was the perky reply.

Ooof! It was as if I'd just caught a solid body shot right in the gut.

Perhaps one of the most lamentable aspects of Occidental culture is a growing tendency to muddle the difference between "truth" and "lie." What used to be a well-defined border clearly separating these eternally warring foes, has now become a disputed territory in a constant state of flux. This war has become so fatiguing in our overly competitive society – where the "truth" has evolved into little more than a self-serving perversion for somebody's hustle – that we've unconsciously set up a new kind of DMZ, or "Demoralized Zone," where the concepts "truth" and "lie" are simply not respected. It's a place where our consciences don't have to come into play and that annoying intruder called "guilt" is set aside. We don't explain it to ourselves in such a way, but we invent euphemisms like "advertising," "spin," "marketing," and yes, "public relations," to deodorize behavior which is nothing more than what we now consider **acceptable lying**. If a Martian were to tap me on the shoulder and ask what "public relations" means, I'd say, "it is a calculated attempt to make some entity or person look better than it really is."

Anything goes in the DMZ.

I write this essay at the height of our political season, the elections of '96 being only weeks away. At this juncture in history, I find it easy to say that our electoral campaigns are fought almost exclusively within the "Demoralized Zone." The concepts "truth" and "lie" have been so obliterated that all we have left is a disorienting pea soup fog lacking any clarity whatsoever. As the incessant political ads bounce off each other like a long rally in a tennis match, those of us who still have enough optimism? naiveté? foolishness? or just plain stubbornness to cast a vote, can only sit back and wonder if the English language can still be used to communicate information. Candidate Slick says something is white; candidate Sly says it is black; and they both go on to perfectly justify themselves and completely discredit their opponent. The difference between black and white, which we used to be very comfortable with, has now been put in doubt. The intellectual process now used to choose a candidate has been reduced almost exclusively to deciding on who is lying the least. We hardly even bother with who might be telling the truth; we don't believe anyone is.

This year's electoral circus has made a celebrity out of a shady political strategist named Dick Morris. Morris was the chief "spin master" for the Clinton campaign when he was caught with an expensive erection and an inappropriate partner. Such an occurrence used to result in public disgrace, but nowadays, inside the DMZ, it means you can laugh it off and become a millionaire by writing a "tell all" book which nobody knows whether to believe or not.

But Morris' escapade was perhaps not in vane. It helped us grunts outside the DMZ to understand the game a bit more.

It seems that Morris was little more than a "hired gun" who'd worked for both liberal and conservative candidates with an equal amount of zeal and lack of scruples. As long as the pay was right, Morris didn't have any political convictions. If the Unabomber were running for office and the deal was finger lickin' juicy enough, he'd make him look like a visionary genius leading us all to salvation. This has left a bad after taste. Is this what we've come to?

Should we really be surprised by this? Flip on the television. It won't be long before a "hired gun" of one sort or another will appear, giving their all for something they have absolutely no emotional attachment to, for something they probably know nothing about. Here's a well-groomed, attractive woman (ugly people are rarely permitted on TV commercials) passionately proclaiming the virtues of a pill for heartburn. Here's a sophisticated English gentleman preaching the fulfillment of your life's quest through the purchase of a certain luxury car. If we are not willing to call these people liars, we can at least admit they are showing a gross indifference for the truth.

Dick Morris is everywhere and we've grown quite comfortable with it.

It might be easy for someone reading this piece to say, "lighten up, c'mon, they're only commercials, how can you find so much evil in such familiar, average, acceptable behavior?" But that's just the point. We don't question these attitudes anymore. We've begun to consider infidelity to the truth as something normal. The concept "truth" has been so devalued that it is now a far cheaper commodity than "what we can make them believe," for which billions of dollars are spent every year. The "Demoralized Zone" is continuing to spread out and claim more territory. We might be approaching a future where it will absorb all the space that used to be occupied by "truth" or "lie," until there will only be the DMZ, which is another way to say "whatever you can get away with."

Is that an emotionally healthy state of being?

Relevant Material: *"If things appear deformed and distorted, it's generally not because of books. It's more because of the movies, the press, the commercials on TV. Above all else, the latter! Who can now say for sure where information ends and where publicity begins (or vice versa)?" From the novel, "Regreso del Infierno" (Return From Hell), by the Spaniard, Jose Ferrater Mora.*

The following quote makes reference to the "Chips" and the "Shops," which are fictional media companies similar to CNN and Fox.) "For two or three days, there were tense relations between the "Chips" and the "Shops," with an endless bombardment of editorials; finally – and this is what they wanted – the public didn't know what to believe." From the classic satire, "La Princesa Durmiente Va a la Escuela" (Sleeping Beauty Goes to School), by the Spanish master, Gonzalo Torrente Ballester.

WHY I HATE THE OLYMPICS

Although I've devoted a good deal of material to the Olympics in this ongoing glacier of philosophical slush, not since Atlanta '96 has the topic appeared in these pages. My previous forays dwelled upon the self-centered xenophobia which, for this pundit, has made the Olympic Movement a patently negative experience for the human race. The Olympics promote peace, harmony and goodwill amongst men in much the same way Spring Break promotes sobriety.

The 2002 Winter Games in Salt Lake City only served to reinforce these feelings. Its personality was so adolescent aggressive that it came close to resurrecting the Cold War. What we have here is war without bullets. The Olympics not only do nothing to lessen our tendencies to engage in real war, they seem to pave the road in that direction. Salt Lake City, excluding the boycotted Games of the 1980's, was probably the worst example of this in my lifetime. (Berlin '36, the Nazi Olympics, might still be King.) Giving oxygen to this fire is that the Olympic Games have become a purely commercial enterprise ... and war sells.

Given the unctuous patriotic goulash America is still wallowing in since 9/11, I tried my best to flee the Games, but its presence was so omnipotent that total escape proved impossible. But let's also fess up: most of the events are wonderful spectacles performed by gifted athletes. I can't remember the last time I actually watched a hockey match, but the style of play at the Olympics is such an artistic triumph compared to the goony mayhem played in the NHL, that watch I did. Most of the other rarely seen forms of skating, skiing and sliding can also make for interesting viewing. It's not the athletic competition I object to, but the emotional climate it is forced to operate in.

The Games ran for 17 days, with NBC providing the television coverage. But this is just one star in a far-flung galaxy of news and information sources. For 17 days, countless news blurbs dealing with the subject, from an exaggerated number of sources, slid through our consciousness. In all that time, I cannot remember one instance where the performance of our American athletes was not the focus of any news item having to do with the Olympics. Did we win? Did we lose? Period. On numerous occasions, an American bronze or silver medalist would be mentioned without telling who won the gold! (I can repeat that if you don't think you heard right). This tunnel vision obsession with our own athletes will come into sharper focus a bit further on, when I discuss the athlete who, without a doubt, was the most extraordinary performer at Salt Lake City 2002.

Being that the United States did better than it ever had at the Winter Games, local coverage had an almost neurotic fixation on the medal count amongst warring nations. One trying to mitigate this success could point to the mother lode of medals carted away by the Yanks in many of the newly invented generation X sports (moguls, flugles, aerial doodlies, ring dings and such), many of which have been created in the United States and still have a limited pool of international participation. Back in the days when the Soviets used to dominate both the Winter and Summer Games, I can remember how we used to scoff at many of the kinky sports they excelled in (bear wrestling, vodka chugging, caviar diving, whatever). Notice how the worm has turned.

This self-centered nationalism is certainly not the exclusive property of the happiest nation ever there was, but there does seem to be a morbid devotion to being #1 in America that seems less relevant elsewhere. It is an integral part of America's identity. Such behavior seems to find its lowest expression at the Olympics and, with the help of America's unchallenged media clout, everyone else begins to resent it. So much for peace, harmony and blah, blah.

If an American "anti-propagandist" (see essay "The Olympic Games") might add some objectivity to this medal count fixation, the following becomes more relevant: Norway, a country with roughly half the population of New York City, won more gold medals than the United States in Salt Lake City.

One day during the Olympics, I was listening to the radio when the five-minute news blurb at the top of the hour came on. ("News" these days seems to be delivered only in blurbs.) The newscaster, with the usual full-bodied, baritone resonance, gravely explained how Dick Cheney was asserting his right to say nothing about anything, something he does with unparalleled talent. Having completed this "blurb," he then went on to explain, with the exact same gravity he had used in the Cheney story, that there had been "great disappointment for the Americans at Salt Lake City." It seems that the woman's curling team had barely been eliminated from medal contention by some frostbitten, yodeling nation of little import. I'm not sure I should admit this, but try as I might, I could not summon up the most minimal smidgen of disappointment necessary for a loyal American. Please don't hate me. I'm not a Taliban. I feel so alienated, so alone amongst so many disappointed Americans.

I sometimes wonder if Cheney would have been bumped into the second slot on the newscast if the curling team had won.

As promised above, I will now discuss the most outstanding athletic performance rendered at Salt Lake City 2002. This athlete performed in an event where the Americans did not medal and, for the most part, did not contend. As a result, anyone who may have experienced these Games in the Disney States of America knows almost nothing of this athlete and what was accomplished. Even more astounding is the fact that this athlete militates in one of the traditional glamour events of the Winter Olympics. We are not talking about moguls, flugles, flips, blips, and new fangled somersaults and circus tricks performed by a limited group of pioneering "dudes" in sports we've never seen before. The sport in question has been around since the first snowfall and has produced famous athletes whose names are well known – with the exception of Botswana – everywhere. Even as I write, I can only blush with embarrassment in admitting that I still don't know the name of this athlete. I'll have to do some research.

One day, near the end of the Games, I came home from work and flipped on the TV. One of the women's alpine skiing events was on. The winner turned out to be a girl from Croatia, which, in itself, is somewhat surprising. Before getting back to her, let's have a word about the amazing athletic accomplishments of this country of only 5 million people: In the last decade or so it has sent numerous basketball players to the NBA, many of whom – Petrovic, Kukoc, many others – have become outstanding players. They won the silver medal in this discipline in Barcelona, finishing only behind the original "Dream Team." Their soccer players have gone out in waves of talent that now ripple through the most important leagues of Europe, many of whom are star players. Their National Team actually reached the semi-finals of a recent World Cup, a remarkable showing. They've produced a Wimbledon champion in Goran Ivanisevic and there are a number of world-class Croatian tennis players, both men and women, playing the sport's top professional tours. If you are still not impressed, it should be mentioned that this was all done while recovering from a brutal civil war that devastated the country. And now, perhaps the most remarkable of all, the skier mentioned at the beginning of this paragraph. She not only won the race I alluded to above, she won by over a second, which, for a sport calibrated in 1/100ths of a second, could be described as lapping the field. While digesting this fact, the announcers mentioned that this was her third gold medal out of a possible four in Alpine Skiing. She seems to have failed miserably in one of these events, having only won silver. (I'm not quite sure what make up the alpine events. An educated guess would be slalom, downhill, giant slalom and combined.)

Just how remarkable was this performance?

I did some research. Alpine skiers, during their season, race on a weekly basis on a World Cup Tour similar to what golfers and tennis players do. It is not usual to find repeat winners from week to week, and multiple winners during the course of the season are limited. It is difficult to dominate this sport. All the skiers are well-trained professionals competing within a heartbeat of each other's skills in a sport as highly evolved and traditional as soccer or baseball. In skiing's long Olympic history, no female has ever done what this Croatian has done, and only one person, the legendary Jean-Claude Killy, skiing at a time when the vast majority of humanity was still not born, has matched it. Considering the magnitude of her accomplishments at one of the world's most high profile events, she should be considered for Athlete of the Year (ESPY's, Sports Illustrated, etc.) and Female Athlete of the Year should be a lock. In American terms, her feats could be compared to winning a Triple Crown in baseball, or rushing for 2000 yards in football. And yet ...

... in the various wrap ups reserved for the few days of post-Olympic glow, I did not see or hear anything about her extraordinary feats. We know about the dudes with their flips and somersaults; we know about the hockey tournament; we know about the American speed skaters who made the transition from Santa Monica skating (a great story); we know about the spoiled brats and whiners in figure skating; we know something about any American who won anything at Salt Lake City ... I ask you ... do you know the name of the Croatian girl who was the best athlete at these Games?

Can you imagine the uproar if an American had done this?

And now I'll tell you why I really hate the Olympics.

Sometime around the mid point of the war games at Salt Lake City, there was a horrific story out of Egypt. It seems there was a train accident where some 370 or so people died. I am certainly not versed in the history of railroad tragedies, but I cannot remember a train wreck that charged such a heavy price in human life. Adding to the magnitude of the tragedy is the way in which it happened: It seems some cars near the back of the train caught fire. The people at the controls, way up at the front, did not become aware of the problem for quite some time and simply went on with their business. Use your imagination. It must have been an infernal disaster.

The next day, the headline on the front page (not the sports page) of USA Today read, "American Women Take Gold in Bobsleigh." (I don't know when "Bobsled" turned into "Bobsleigh," though I must admit my less than rudimentary knowledge of the sport. I think gravity plays a big role in it. Could they be two different sports?) Even if this historic railroad disaster had not taken place on the same day as America's feminine triumph in the "Bobsleigh," I find this headline somewhat puzzling. I feel a bit like Rip Van Winkle. When did the Bobsleigh begin to claim such an important piece of the American consciousness? Did I miss something? I'll have to get out a bit more.

Upon explaining these thoughts to a friend, I was told this Bobsleigh thing carried a bit more media weight because one of the riders was a black girl. She was the first woman of her kind to ever win a gold medal in the Winter Games. Forgive me, but I don't see an Afro-American being used like a sack of potatoes on a sleigh ride as a great triumph for the civil rights movement.

But there is irony here. Although the participation of a person of color made the bobsleigh story more relevant in America, the fact that the hundreds of people who perished in Egypt were also of color, probably made it less newsworthy in America.

The best idea I've ever heard with regard to the Olympic Games came from an elderly Portuguese gentleman named Jose Saramago. His intellectual brilliance and literary talent were recently rewarded with a Nobel Prize for literature. He feels that no country involved in any war, directly or indirectly, should be allowed to participate in the Olympics.

Amen.

P.S.- I have a sorry confession to make. I had a friend of mine look up the name of the Croatian skier. The next day he gave me a print out with all the information on her. Before finishing this essay, I lost it. I'm not going to ask him to do it again. My memory says Kostolic ... or Kostolicic? Her first name is completely gone. Considering the coverage given her feats in America, it seems fitting for it to end this way.

GEORGE W. GIVES A PRESS CONFERENCE

One of the foremost requirements of any mouthpiece for the Real World Order is the ability to lie with grace and sincerity. Although it might seem contradictory, such a person could be described as a "sincere liar." In order to illustrate this, let's construct the following hypothetical situation:

About ten days into Operation Iraqi Freedom, the President is in his room preparing to give a press conference (as you can see, this is very hypothetical). A terrorist has infiltrated the government's inner circle as a domestic servant. While preparing the President a glass of water, he drops a healthy dose of "truth serum" into the clear liquid. Fifteen minutes later George W. stands before the press corp.

The President points to Tom Brokaw of NBC.

"Yes Tom?"

"Mr. President, does it concern you at all that our forces seem to have let Saddam Hussein slip through their hands?"

"No, not really. It would be nice to catch him and parade him around like some trophy fish from my dad's next marlin tournament, but other than that ... no big deal."

"But isn't he a wicked dictator responsible for the suffering of the Iraqi people and ... ?"

The President cuts in ... "Look, Tom, people like Saddam are a dime a dozen. There are lots of Saddams all over the third world. If they cooperate, they are our friends. Do you remember during the campaign when someone asked me where Uzbekistan was?"

Brokaw pauses, his face scrunched in thought. "Actually, I think you were asked who the President of Uzbekistan was?"

The President shrugs. "President, Shmesident ... at the time I knew more about the mating habits of the Texas aardvark than Uzbekistan." The room fills with laughter. When it subsides, he continues. "Well now I know a lot about the President of Uzbekistan. He's a grease ball dictator who let us use his country to launch the attack on Afghanistan. Ergo, he's a good guy. If he crosses us, he'll be considered the grease ball dictator he is and he'll get the Noriega-Saddam treatment."

The room is abuzz with incredulous whispering and gesticulations. Stupefied expressions are everywhere. People are hurriedly playing back their tape recorders just to see if they heard what they thought they did. Peter Jennings of ABC news is the first to recover.

"Mr. President ...Mr. President!"

"Yes Peter."

"So far, no substantial amounts of weapons of mass destruction have been found. Do you still expect to find some?"

The President sighs tiredly, puts his hand over his eyes and shakes his head. He talks without even removing his hand. "*Weapons of mass destruction.*" He removes his hand and stares at the crowd. "It has a nice ring to it, doesn't it?"

"There are none?"

The President looks directly at Jennings as if he were explaining to a child that there is no Santa Claus. "Look, Peter, Saddam Hussein would have a hard time winning a turf war in East L.A."

For a few frozen moments there is stunned silence. The tension then explodes in a chaotic frenzy of shouting, jostling, hand raising, all trying to get the President to respond to them. The room has an anarchic quality reminiscent of the floor of any stock exchange or commodity market.

"Mr. President!"

"Mr. President!"

The President raises his hand and asks for silence. "Mr. President!" The ambiance slowly returns to normal. Bush continues. "Look, there are probably some weapons of mass destruction, but hey, even the Mayberry Police Department has some ..." he pauses, almost tasting his next few words, which he says with sarcastic elegance, "weapons of mass destruction." He looks dreamily out over the gathering, almost blissfully. "I love that phrase. I think Rumsfeld thought of that one."

Once again, the room is convulsed in that commodity market mayhem. Everyone is disoriented, confused.

"Mr. President!"

"Mr. President!"

This time George W. pounds his fist on the podium and shouts, "Hey!!"

The mob has been startled into compliance. The President scans the room. Mouths are agape, eyes are wide open, unfocused, as if they've all just seen a ghost. The silence is eerie, tense, almost touchable.

"Anything else?"

Dan Rather of CBS blinks his eyes and comes out of it. "Uhh ... Mr. President ... do you think ..." He is still too dumbfounded to continue.

"Yes, Dan ...?"

"Uhm ... will we be able to install a democratic regime in Iraq, with freedom and liberty ... and ..." his voice trails off in confusion.

The President tries to help, "... and all that stuff?"

"Yes, and all that stuff."

Bush throws his head back and bursts out laughing. "Oh yes ..." he chuckles a bit more, "*nation building*. I think Condoleezza thought of that one ... or was it Clinton and his gang of fornicators? It has the woman's touch, don't you think? Maybe that tramp Hillary thought of it?"

There is no response. The mob has now gone into a state of incoherent exhaustion, not unlike a beaten fighter sitting on his stool just after the fight has been stopped. There are empty stares, loosened ties, running make up, a general state of stupefaction and rudderless confusion, as if the end of the empire were near.

"Anyone else?"

Rather stares at the ground and mumbles, "But what about democracy?"

"Democracy? Have you noticed the state of democracy in America? Who got more votes in the last election?" Silence. "And you guys ... Tom, Peter, Dan ... c'mon, how long have you been watching the likes of me? You're not buying that crap, are you?" The 3 stars of big media news look at each other, confused, trying to make sense of it all. The President continues, "but the stations you work for have cars and sneakers to sell and you get paid well and everyone knows where their bread is buttered." Silence. With mock mirth, Bush does a Hitler-like jig and chants, "the troops, the troops, our glorious troops ..."

Bill O'Reilly, the star of Fox News and perhaps the brightest color in the crayon box, will have no more of it. "Mr. President, please, explain yourself. None of this is in harmony with anything you've said before about this war. If it is not democracy, or Saddam, or weapons of mass destruction, or ... whatever, why this war?"

"C'mon Bill, you work for that fascist Murdoch. You, more than anyone, know what this is all about."

O'Reilly is stunned. "But ..."

"But what?" The President turns to the main camera in front of him and speaks to the American people, as if this were a speech and not a press conference. "My fellow Americans, I stand before you not to ask your support for this war – because we're gonna' do it anyway, no matter what you tree huggin' sissies think – but to make you understand that we have a global economy to run, and if you want that new SUV next year ... and I hear they'll be bigger than ever, and you know you want one, not to mention the latest DVD-video doo-hickey your kids nag you for, and the super titanium hit-it-to-the-moon golf club ... in short, all the stuff that makes our way of life – that's right, you heard it! our sacred, Christian-Judeo way of life ... and I think it's about time we put the Christian ahead of the Judeo ... My fellow Americans, we need that oil! We can't have some goddam towel head turning the faucet on and off for us. You will not be happy until we have this oil. It is my job to make you happy ... or at least enough of you to keep my guys in office ... and me rich. **God Bless America!**"

LETTER TO A DEAD SOLDIER'S MOTHER

(11/04)

This essay is a reaction to a piece recently presented on National Public Radio. My patience with Public Broadcasting was already on the brink of exhaustion when the story in question pushed it into the abyss of informational sources not worth taking seriously. This is a particularly stinging blow for an American truth seeker, because Public Broadcasting might have been the last mainstream media source where some facsimile of reality was still available. Obviously, the pressures of raising money, with its ever-growing dependence on large corporate donors, has now coerced Public Broadcasting's message within the narrow bounds set forth by the global practitioners.

The piece in question could only be deemed a quintessential cliché. We were taken to 3 rural towns – a place in Maryland whose name never stuck; another town called Covington, La.; and Laramie, Wyo., a place less anonymous but surely a similar hotbed of stunted, provincial intellect. In each case, a young soldier had recently died in Iraq and we were made privy to the comments of his family and townsfolk. What followed was a flood tide of icky goo as they remembered the fallen hero as a wonderful this, or a friendly that, as a good son or magnetic blah, blah, as a gentle yak, yak, a loveable badda boom, always ready with a joke or a good natured yadda, yadda, as a star pitcher and a tear here and there, with droves of flowers and prayers and scholarships in his name and ... get the picture? You've seen this one? A hundred times.

The piece ran for about 15 minutes. Conspicuously absent was any angst with regard to the war's necessity or validity. The deaths of these young soldiers were accepted in the same way one would accept a drop in temperature on a north wind. The last segment – the one from Laramie – set off my *I can't stand it anymore* alarm, leading to a brusque shutting off of the radio and the eventual appearance of this essay. It seems that the mother of the dead soldier had received a letter or E-mail where he said, " ... mother, you can't imagine how bad it is to live under a dictator. We have to defend our freedom ..." and other such pearls of teenage wisdom. Could Goebbels do it any better?

I don't doubt that the people used in this story were genuine and sincere. An effective propaganda source does not have to artificially concoct a theatrical version of the message they want to create. But they can selectively decide what to highlight and sell. They are always giving us the actress in the light she looks the best in. We will never see her as she gets out of bed in the morning, with her rancid breath, disheveled hair and pale, blemished skin. This latest Bush Oil War is trying to convince us that Elizabeth Taylor is still sexy and the whole studio is working overtime to do it. The question is: how gullible are the viewers?

This writer does not work for the studio. That means he can write the following letter of condolence to the mother of that dead soldier in Laramie, Wyo.:

Dear Dead Soldier's Mother,

I heard your interview on National Public Radio pertaining to your son's death and found it so disturbing that I could not help but write this letter as a meager way to purge my anger. I realize it will probably not be what you want to hear, but I send it off anyway with the remote hope that it might awaken some dormant seed of intellectual capability that surely lurks deeply buried in the physiology of your being. Unfortunately, it is infinitely more probable it will arouse your fears and anger, two human traits that have been far more cultivated by the people responsible for your son's death. With this in mind, and before going one word further, please accept – in spite of how you might feel about me after reading this letter – my most heartfelt sympathy for the death of your son. One of the most basic instincts of life is to procreate and a parent having to bury a child can only be recognized as one of the truest sorrows a human being can experience. I hope you can remember the genuine grief I feel for you as you continue reading this letter.

And now comes the hard part. Your son, Mrs. Dead Soldier's Mother, died in vain. In spite of what he may have thought, he did not die fighting for my freedom, your freedom, or anyone else's freedom. He was not defending our country, or spreading democracy, or ridding a foreign land of a cruel dictator, and to say he was "liberating" the Iraqi people is a disgusting joke beyond the realm of any decency. He was nothing more than a pawn used in a dirty imperial game meant to secure a natural resource coveted by those responsible for his death. If your habitual sources of information have not expressed it to you in such a way, it is because they are co-conspirators in the usurpation and death of your son.

A traditional factor leading to the grief you are suffering is an insufficient intellectual base with which to defend yourself from such usurpation. Please don't misunderstand me. By emphasizing such intellectual weakness, I don't mean to suggest that you or your son are/were stupid. Although human beings might have differing interests and talents, we are all born, with rare exceptions, with similar reasoning capacities, with similar capabilities to think, deduce, and process the data our life experience comes in contact with. What differs greatly amongst us is this life experience and where it leads us. For millions of people, this life experience could be dubbed as "data deficient," because their information sources, as well as their ability and/or zeal in pursuing useful data, are limited. Much of this has to do with that whole tangled web of sociological muck we refer to as "social class," a quagmire definitely not appropriate for this letter and surely beyond the scope your own life experience has offered you. With this in mind, let me put it to you like this:

It is my guess, Mrs. Dead Soldier's Mother, that you are not an affluent person. You may not be desperately poor – though it is quite probable that many of the men in

Iraq seeing true combat come from such deprived environments – but I'd sooner think to go snow skiing in the Amazon before I'd think you are affluent. You know why? Because affluent people are not getting killed in Iraq. Affluent people are sitting home thanking your dead son for his great sacrifice while watching football games rife with patriotic symbols and rhetoric. That includes your President, whom, in your data starved confusion, I'm reasonably certain you voted for. If you are offended or upset with this paragraph, I suggest the following course of action:

Turn off the TV – the "reality shows," the soap operas, the gossip mongering, brain killing talk shows and such – and go do some research into the military careers of the President and his most trusted advisors ... the one's who sent your son off to his death. Go ahead, it won't take long because almost all of them have no military records. That's right, Mrs. Dead Soldier's Mother, virtually none of them have ever faced one hostile bullet in their whole lives. And guess what? They are all very affluent. You know what I'd be willing to bet? I'd bet that none of their sons are fighting in Iraq either.

But this is not a rant about rich and poor, or what the Republicans would call "class warfare." If some people have swimming pools twice the size of most peoples' apartments, I can live with that. If you really want that swimming pool, there are enough avenues open in our society to procure it. But when people are asked to go off and die in defense of that swimming pool there can be no divisions of labor. Everyone – poor, rich, and in between – must assume equal parts in this burden. If dying is not shared communally by the whole nation, then no war can ever be considered a just war.

I know it will hurt you, Mrs. Dead Soldier's Mother, when I say that your son and almost all the soldiers he fought with were not motivated by patriotic fervor or love of country. Most of them, like your son, were just a bunch of teenagers fresh out of high school, looking for something to do with their lives. The military offered them some security in a difficult world: a place to live, some food to eat, some money to spend, a chance to get out of the stultifying reality of their meager world experience, and the recruiter surely made it sound pretty good. Heck, a lot of them probably even thought that a dose of war could be a great adventure. They'd seen all the films by Mel Gibson, and Schwarzenegger, and Bruce Willis and all the rest, and they thought, "Hey, I'd like a piece of that." Did you ever stop to think that not one of these Hollywood heroes – not <u>one</u>, Mrs. Dead Soldier's Mother – has ever come near a real bullet aimed at them? That's right, not even John Wayne. They are a lot like Bush-Cheney and all their cronies in that respect ... and to top it all off, they get paid millions of dollars to fake it, while your son got paid peanuts to really die.

Oh yes, the truth must eventually be told and if this letter can have an impact on you and the others like you, Mrs. Dead Soldier's Mother, then your son's death will not have been in vain.

There is one positive thing I can say about your son and it gives me great pleasure in saying it to you: your son was not a coward. This is a wonderful testimony in today's America because our nation, taken as a whole, has become a very cowardly nation. We are taking the immense wealth of our country – a wealth we can be proud of – and squandering it on obscene military expenditures that are sucking the life out of an ever-weakening social contract needed to better serve its people and the world. And what do we do with these billions of dollars in military power, an investment that is almost more than the rest of the world combined? We attack little third world countries in pursuit of our imperial global economy needs. That's right, Mrs. Dead Soldier's Mother, it's not freedom or democracy, it's a killing spree meant to maintain and perpetrate their diarrhea of fat ass consumption, and millions and millions of Americans sit back and applaud these efforts because they have your son out there dying for them.

Don't you think they're a bunch of cowards, Mrs. Dead Soldier's Mother?

OK, enough. I'm sorry if I've upset you, but I suppose there's a slim chance these thoughts are opening your mind to the supreme crime you and your son have been the victim of ... but I doubt it. It's more likely that you hate me by now and are greatly offended by this letter. If such is the case, I ask you to consider this: my grief for your son's death is infinitely more genuine than the cowards running our government who sent him out to die. This is no form letter from your draft-dodging President. I took a lot of time to write it.

Sincerely,
Post Consumer Man

PCM INTERVIEWS W.

(12/06)

After 6 years of the agglomeration we call the George W. Bush administration, and almost 4 years of the horrifying cesspool we call the war in Iraq, this essay cannot be called an exercise in entirely new material. Our mainstream media's lack of sincerity in pursuing the hard-core reality of this war's instigation has been touched upon before in these pages (see all the "Propaganda" essays, and more). With the war now going so obviously down the toilet, the W. government has had to endure a withering media assault on its policies that could make the previous media insincerity seem irrelevant. I'm here to remind you it is just the opposite.

As the burlesque of the war and the media's coverage of it stretches on into eternity, the ludicrous performance of our "free press" has become even more insincere. One must remember that America's "Big Media" establishment had no trouble leading us gleefully into the fray. Now that the war has become the arthritic old nag it is, Big Media's disengagement and criticism of it still lacks the courage to ask the fundamental questions; still refuses to go for the jugular; still refuses to be sincere with its constituents. It is now more relevant than ever to further delve into these matters.

In order to illustrate this, I will now give America the interview it will never see or hear on Big Media, the one we should all hear, the only one that counts (and that is why it will only appear here).

PCM - First off, Mr. President, I'd like to not thank you for this interview. We all know it only exists on these pages and nowhere else, thus emaciating its impact to an almost negligible extent. We all know you'd never ever agree to this interview in reality, so no thanks for nothing.

W. - (with that manure-shoveling grin we've all grown to know) You're not welcome. I may be stupid as bottled barbecue sauce, but I'm not nuts.

PCM - And what you've done in Iraq is not nuts?

W. - No, no, that was just an error. With all the Nintendo game weapons we have, who'd a thunk it? Now those Ayrabs – they are really nuts! They're almost as crazy as me giving you a real interview, but we know that will never happen. That nuts I'm not.

PCM - I suppose not.

W. - (leaning forward and touching PCM on the knee) By the way, you are –?

PCM - Post Consumer Man.

W. - Oh, right. Look, Mr. Man, can I call you Post? You know how I like to have a good natured, friendly rapport with the Press Corp.

PCM - Sure. In truth, you're very good with a quip and a joke. Just think how much better you'd have been for America as a comedian than as president.

W. - I'll take that as a compliment, Post.

PCM - (arranging notes, clearing throat, getting serious) OK, let's get to the meat of it all.

W. - Fire away.

PCM - Mr. President, one of the most consistent ideas you've held forth through this whole war is that we will not leave until the mission is completed. Could you please explain what the mission is?

W. - Of course. The mission is to provide a stable, democratic government in Iraq, one where the Iraqi people can live in freedom.

(Author's note - In the real world, this is the point where Big Media and its news and information shows with the most hegemony over public opinion, purposely drop the ball. In spite of all their resources, technology, reporters and pundits debating and analyzing the war in all its minutia, it leaves the most basic, fundamental question of "why?" at this ridiculously superficial level, leaving it to voiceless people like PCM to ask the real questions in hypothetical interviews like this. With regard to the W. Bush presidency and its war in Iraq, Big Media has failed the American people in every way, contributing immensely to the tragedy we now all own).

PCM - I don't remember an outpouring of grief from within Iraq asking us to "free" them. I mean, who asked us to do this?

W. - (smiling radiantly) Ahh, the yearning to be free is a universal feeling in the spirit of mankind. Nobody had to ask us, Post, we could feel its heartbeat, even from 6,000 miles away.

PCM - But Mr. President, we are approaching the half trillion-dollar mark in expenditures here, with no end in sight. If the mission is to simply free and democratize a country, do you consider that cost effective?

W. - You can't put a price on freedom, Post.

PCM - OK, well – if that's the case, there must be 100 countries all over the world ruled by despotic tyrants who brutalize their people, crush all opposition, many times leading to genocidal butchery or horrendous civil wars. Why did you choose to democratize Iraq instead of – let's say, Sudan, where our intervention may have truly done some good?

W. - Hey, first off, we're doing plenty good in Iraq –

PCM - – Mr. President, what I see from Iraq would humble my worst nightmares –

W. - – and we're aware of the situation in Dar – Dar –

PCM - Darfur.

W. - Right – and we'll do all we can, but we are tied up a bit right now.

PCM - Let's get back to this democracy thing.

W. - Yes, I love democracy.

PCM - When it comes to the Middle East, all of our client states, like Kuwait, Saudi Arabia –

W. - (breaking in) Hold it, hold it. They are not "client" states, they are "allies."

PCM - Suit yourself. In any event, Kuwait, the Saudis, the Gulf States, etc. – none of them are even remotely democratic, while the country you've demonized and threatened over and over again, Iran, just held a legitimate election and seems to have a somewhat rooted democracy.

W. - Yeah, but the religious freaks in the turbans run everything.

PCM - Maybe. I don't claim to be an expert on Iranian affairs, but it certainly looks as if they have some form of a democratic tradition far more robust than our "allies" in the region.

W. - Yes, but their government's policies are contrary to our interests.

PCM - Ah hah! So it's not democracy, it's more a question of who is playing ball with us or not, right?

W. - Now hold on, I didn't say that –

PCM - I'll give you another example of this from our own hemisphere. Have you heard the name Hugo Chavez?

W. - C'mon Post, I'm the president, I'm up on these things.

PCM - Well, you've demonized Chavez as much as anyone in the world and he's been democratically elected more times than you with far greater margins.

W - Yeah, but he stood up in front of the world and called me a devil and acted like I smell bad!

PCM - Not before you engineered a coup in a very undemocratic effort to remove him from office –

W. - (angry) Now hold it –

PCM - – and bungled that too!

W. - – You have no proof of that!

PCM - (shouting) And can you prove you are not the devil?

W. - (shouting back) I can prove I don't smell bad!

PCM - –

W. - –

PCM - –

W. - (arranging his cuff links, smoothing his hair, composing self) You see Post, this is why you'll never have a real interview with me, why you have to fake it here in one of your essays, why I only talk to guys like Wolf Blitzer.

PCM - That may be true, but there is one advantage I have; you can't escape, you are going to have to fess up, something Wolf and the boys and girls never make you do.

W. - (shrugging) Big deal. Go ahead.

PCM - Now, if Chavez has been democratically elected and you value democracy so much, why do you demonize him so?

W. - Are you kidding? He hangs around with Fidel Castro, he's a friggin' commie.

PCM - Ah hah! Once again, you show you are more interested in who is playing ball with us, and not in democracy.

W. - Well, it's not that simple. It's a combination of things. You have to think of our national interest too.

PCM - I'm glad you brought that up.

W. - Uh oh.

PCM - What exactly is our national interest in Iraq? The security threat was either a complete lie or a complete mistake, and yet you persist in this mission to stabilize and democratize. Let me put it to you like this –

W. - Do you have to?

PCM - Somebody's gotta do it.

W. - Well, it might as well be you – much better than Wolf Blitzer.

PCM - Right. This is what all the Wolf Blitzers scattered all over the Big Media television dial will not ask you. Mr. President, if the most rentable product in Iraq was – asparagus, would you be interested in democratizing and "freeing" the country?

W. - (in a weak voice) Maybe. I like asparagus.

PCM - Is it worth a half a trillion dollars and more to keep the price of asparagus down?

W. - Well – I'd have to run it by my advisors.

PCM - I'll take that as a "no." Let's face it, a half trillion and more is a pretty steep price, even for oil.

W. - Yeah, more than we expected, and it makes it so damn hard to leave.

PCM - You mean it's hard to just leave all that oil there after all this?

W. - I'm not going there, and not even you can make me do it.

PCM - Perhaps it's not necessary at this point. Once again, no thanks for nothing, and may you and your whole team rot in Hell.

W. - You don't really believe in that, do you?

Relevant Material: *Two days before the mid term elections of 2006, President Bush, campaigning before friendly fire and in an obvious rut of desperation, talked about Iraq and the danger of not succeeding, mentioning the national interest of the area's oil deposits. He even talked about the price of oil and what could happen if – etc., etc. I saw news footage of these comments shortly after he'd said them. It seemed so out of character for him to mention the "o" word, I expected the media to jump all over it. With the exception of Keith Olbermann, who did make a big deal of it on his nightly news show, the rest of the press corp must have been out playing golf, for there was nary a word about it from anywhere else in Big Media's realm. In fact, Olbermann's rant was rife with questions as to why this was so.*

TERRORISM, I

(4/08)

There are a number of things about the contemporary brand of terrorism – its “modus operandi,” etc. – that seem not just peculiar, but suspicious in nature, suspicious in the sense that its sincerity might even be called into question. Some of the questions I will raise in the following essay (see essay, “Terrorism, II“) could even suggest a conscious lack of optimal effectiveness, thus leading to conspiracy theories with regard to who are truly enemies in the global economic struggle that is the trigger for all geo-political action in the world.

Terrorism is nothing new. Although we now associate the word with hawk-billed Moslems, peering out gaunt with hate from under Middle Eastern head garb, any number of allegedly aggrieved groups operating from a position of military weakness, have resorted to such tactics. Still fresh in historic memory is the “Cubana” plane blown up by Cuban exiles over Venezuela, or the libertarian Americans who destroyed the federal building in Oklahoma, without even mentioning such institutional-habituals as the I.R.A. operating in the British Isles, or the militant arm of Basque separatism, ETA. This represents a micro-list of similar behavior that could fill a thick volume.

Today’s most prominent version of terrorism is sprung from the gargantuan energy needs caused by the

Occidental idea of an economic system. The source of this energy is found most abundantly in Moslem lands. The procurement of this raw material has created enough western interference in the exploited lands to antagonize a large segment of the Arab and Moslem world. Throw in the added insult of the creation of Israel in what had been a Moslem stronghold for more than 1000 years (in truth, without the oil resources nearby, I doubt if the Zionist idea would have ever been brokered), and you've created a boiling stew of anger whose military capabilities are, at best, piddling compared to the perceived aggressors. This is a perfect ecosystem for the incubation of terrorism.

The Islamic terrorists had signed their signature to many acts of aggression before 9/11, but the spectacular events of that day crossed an emotional frontier that was exploited with ease by an adolescent, headstrong Bush Administration with imperial designs far beyond its predecessors. One would have to go back to Teddy Roosevelt to find an American government with such imperial zeal.

The crossing of this emotional frontier could be attributed to a number of things: the spectacular magnitude of the event; the fact that it happened on American soil, even though a similar attack took place at the same site less than a decade before; the geo-political situation it was sprung from. Undoubtedly, the accumulation of all these things contributed to the collective mentality necessary for the second Bush Oil War, but for this writer, the circumstance of how the event unfolded was the determining factor.

Would anyone dispute that the aerial assault on the Twin Towers and their subsequent collapse was the most photogenic news story in history? Perhaps its closest relative in this kind of genealogy would be the explosion of the great air ship, the Hindenburg. Our memories have been etched forever with the brilliant play by play of that bygone newscaster. The spontaneity of his genuine grief and dismay have still not been forgotten.

The Hindenburg disaster, being the spin off of a scheduled event in an accessible place, was visually recorded. The same cannot be said for the spectacular Titanic disaster, whose photogenity and scope could actually rival the Twin Towers episode. It's legacy not only never seems to die, but continues to grow. Hardly ten years go by without another extravagant Hollywood production adding to its legend – the icy clear night, the windless flat sea, the kaleidoscope of stars, the severe angle with which the behemoth vessel slid to its final resting place. All this conspired in creating an image that seems impervious to both indifference and Alzheimer's.

But alas! It took place in a technologically simpler time. Correct me if I'm wrong, but there seems to be no motion picture documentation of the tragedy. Obviously, there are excellent first hand accounts, but almost all of humanity has only seen representations of it, not the real thing.

If we update the technology to the year 2001, and match such to the events of 9/11, we have finally seen created the "perfect storm" of visually recorded news events. All the stars lined up militarily to give us a pictorial representation thought only possible in the fictional world of Hollywood moguls, and we were seeing it **as it happened**, as if we were spectators at a sporting event. It became another kind of "where were you" milestone in the same vein as Pearl Harbor or JFK, but we saw it not just as consumers of news, but as live onlookers. I can still remember my mother coming out of her bedroom (I was visiting at the time), somewhat confused and unsure, and saying that a plane had just flown into the World Trade Center. A big plane? An accident? Who? We adjourned to the TV screen where a nasty gash filled with flames had deeply scarred the upper reaches of the skyscraper. Thick plumes of dark smoke were already painted across the perfect blue sky of that beautiful late summer day.

By then, just like my mom and I, millions of Americans must have been watching. In other words, the huge crowd was still filing in as the first inning ended. No one could imagine what an unbelievable game it would turn out to be.

There is no need to refresh anyone's memory here. If you saw the events of that day, you'd now have to be dead or certifiably mentally incapacitated to not remember. (The murder of Lee Harvey Oswald has a similar spontaneous quality, but its audience and visual grandeur cannot be mentioned along side 9/11.)

The 9/11 spectacle marked a new era not so much in terrorism (in truth, not much has changed in that forum) but the way in which it is treated in the public arena. Although it had always been on the team, it now became the super star in the political lineup of our day. How a candidate relates to this issue is quite possibly the strongest or weakest political currency he or she can have.

Is one weak or strong on terrorism? Can this person protect us from terrorism? – and other such simple-minded banalities, now permeate our electoral burlesque. It is a "fool's gold" kind of issue that can decide who becomes the Fearless Leader of the world's only Stupid Power.

It is easy to say that the geo-political facts of our times made 9/11 the blockbuster video it will always be. But the amazing set of circumstances which provided for an almost unanimous TV audience already in place to watch such spectacular real "theater" as it happened is unprecedented. It had a major role in creating the hysterical climate which paved the way for the extraordinary blunders of an American government adept at propaganda, but woefully short on policy intellect. The visual imagery associated with 9/11 probably had a greater influence on the future than the geo-political reality it took place in. We didn't just hear about it or see film of it later – we actually lived it. For Big Media, it was their walk-off home run in the 7th game of the World Series.

Which brings me to – "Terrorism, II."

TERRORISM, II

(4/08. This essay is the companion to "Terrorism, I" and should be read with it.)

The events spoken of in the previous essay quite logically upped the ante with regard to "terrorism." It now became a hyper-conscious element in the American mind set. The paranoia level was not only naturally increased by all this, but consciously stimulated by political interests taking advantage of it. The somewhat "Hitlerian" term, the "homeland," made its debut in American patriotic rhetoric. Protecting the "homeland" has now become fashionable terminology, much like the word "dude" has become a signature word for our younger generations. "Hey dude, have you heard about the new Department of *Homeland* Security?" In the same way the weatherman gives us a daily rundown of air quality (good, not so good, don't breathe), we now awake to a daily color code for terrorist danger – yellow (you can go play golf); orange (you can go out, but carry a baseball bat); red (lock the door and hide under your bed). **TERRORISM!** They are out to get us. Watch your neighbor, report anything suspicious, do you know anyone named Abdul?

But whatever you do, do not, I repeat, do not stop shopping. We'll show them.

And yet, regardless of this emotional escalation, we seem no more "terrorized" now than we did before all this happened. As the old saying goes, "shit happens," and it could very well happen again, but the general level of such terrorist behavior – its rhythm, its tenor, its metaphysical presence in the atmosphere – has changed very little, not just since 9/11, but going back 15 to 20 years. This seems puzzling for a number of reasons.

Although, as I write, this essay was born just yesterday, its conceptive womb-spark occurred 10 months before while on my beloved island in the Spanish Mediterranean. The local airport, which is the hub for a thriving tourist industry, is a fairly large one that services thousands of direct charter flights from all over northern Europe. One day, it received a bomb threat. By now we all know the ritual: thousands of people were evacuated from the premises for many hours. It was hot, there was little shade, and the merciless Hellenic-Roman sun beat down like a sledgehammer on the ghostly white northerners. The local forces of law and order, as well as the various agencies of health and sanitation, had to be mobilized. Hundreds of flights were disrupted and some facsimile of normalcy did not return for days.

That's right, the usual chaos such an occurrence engenders.

One has to wonder why these bomb threats do not happen more often? With a minimal amount of risk, those interested in bringing down the Occidental world could inflict such wounds with a methodical jab-jab-jab to an eventually bloodied, worn down, swollen-faced target. The economic system, which is the centerpiece of the Anglo-Euro concept of happiness, would be severely stressed in dealing with such disruptions. It would seem easy pickings for the enemies of the developed world.

Who knows, perhaps the authorities have begun to ignore the vast majority of these threats, but if we cast aside such theater and dwell upon the kind of real death and destruction a terrorist could so easily inflict – and quite possibly with impunity – the peculiar lack of such action becomes a head-scratching riddle.

Two months after this essay's womb-spark, its development was accelerated further by the following circumstances: Every September, I go north to visit my family. The last weekend of such is always reserved for a stay at a sibling's summer home on one of those duney-beachy barrier islands that are so heavenly beautiful in the summer, the kind of island where, in the movies, adolescent boys have virginal affairs with bored, experienced women. Like all vacation spots of this kind that are worth a damn, one must get there by ferry.

Everyday, for about 4 to 5 months, perhaps as many as 50 trips are made between the various points of connection. Each boat will carry up to 200 people, crossing and re-crossing in an endless Ping-Pong of transportation. The terminal on the mainland is not extravagant, but it is swarming with hundreds of people at almost all times of the day. In addition, there is a vast plain of parking whose closest vehicles can be parked no more than 30 yards from the terminal.

In all this landscape of care free summer fun and relaxation, there is not the faintest hint of a security presence anywhere – not in or around the terminal; not while boarding the boats; not in entering the parking lot.

Both on the boats and in the terminal, there is luggage strewn about carelessly, usually the kind of weekender handbag pieces that could be so convenient in carrying an explosive device. Nobody ever checks any of this. An early bird SUV with a similar cargo as that which destroyed the federal building in Oklahoma, could be anonymously parked well within super destructive range.

Get the picture?

In such an environment of "lazy, hazy, crazy days of summer," where everyone's guard seems to be completely down, there'd be no need for suicide bombers and other such fanaticisms. Get in, get out, get away, **boom!** Hundreds are horribly killed. Some radical group claims responsibility. America is shaken down to the pith of its marrow. Die infidels, we will do it again soon.

How many places do you know like this? Look around. The easily attacked targets could almost be called infinite. A similar run of attacks would have as much impact as the more spectacular but singular strike on 9/11. They are amongst us. When will they do it again? I'm not going out.

Once again, I ask the obvious question: why not? Operations of this nature not only would not need high levels of expertise nor elaborate planning, they would require very little in funding.

There is no need to pretend I have an adequate response to this question. And that is why this all seems so peculiar. The most obvious answer would be the fear of a massive, unified, Occidental military response to a serial string of terrorist attacks. But whom do you attack? It is relevant to mention here that the invasion of Iraq was not premised upon a response to terrorism. That was only a pretense, the securing of a natural resource being the true catalyst. If an attempt to quell terrorism is the sincere goal, do you simply declare war on the whole Arab-Moslem world and try to militarily subdue it all? Is that a reasonable expectation? Can it be paid for? Might it not be the same trap the Americans have fallen into in Iraq on a grander scale? And the nuclear option? Can you start killing hundreds of thousands of people for the actions of a handful of desperados?

None of this seems feasible. In fact, it could even play into the hands of the fundamentalist zealots – a showdown, on their turf, on their terms.

It makes you wonder why – why aren't there more terrorist attacks?

ISRAELIS AND PALESTINIANS REVISITED

(5/08, Spain)

Way back in 2001, I wrote the essay "Israelis and Palestinians." For an American, and even more so for a Jew, it did not whistle the usual Dixie with regard to the pretenses under which the Jewish state was born. Almost all my relatives would consider my remarks as nothing more than blasphemous treason, thus making it far more convenient if the essay found its niche in unread obscurity amongst this group. As for the rest of the 6 billion or so human organisms now terrorizing this planet, my desire to have anything I write be read still stands, so go ahead.

2008 is the 60th anniversary of the creation of Israel, its birth being on May 15, 1948. This milestone was surely the genesis of a long editorial page article that appeared in one of the local newspapers where I reside by the Roman Sea. In an occidental, Judeo-Christian nation like Spain, one would expect such an anniversary to be met with the usual back slapping congratulations for a job well done, way to go, keep up the good work, and many more to come, rah, rah, rah, yea Israel!

And that is why the title of the piece, "Israel: The Myths of a Nation," caught my eye. There was a touch of negativity here that led me to glance at its content, just to see if the party line was perhaps being deviated from.

I'll say!

It is relevant to note the publication in question is your average daily newspaper, the kind of thing that would plunk against your front door in America if the paperboy has a good arm. Over the years, I've come to know it as a fairly normal source of Anglo-Euro spin. In no way can it be considered a mouthpiece for an Islamic point of view, nor any other radical concept one might conjure up. In spite of that, I found myself reading a scholarly article that could never appear in a mainstream American print or electronic news outlet. Once again, the overly filtered, narrow nature of information (propaganda?) in the United States was being revealed.

As I explain in the Introduction to this book of essays, I am not an "expert" on anything. My voice is meant to be a generic voice, the thoughts of Citizen X trying to put all the stimuli around him into some kind of cohesive, rational order with which to base his feelings and actions upon. In my attempts to most clearly focus these feelings (that is, to try and be correct), I will seek the most stimuli sources possible – literature, travel, a second language, artistic discovery, the visual arts, imbursements in articles like the one now under discussion, philosophical and scientific non-fiction, contact and debate with others increasing their stimuli base – anything that might feed a healthy intellectual curiosity. The purpose of these essays is to try and decipher what goes on around us through the eyes of someone using almost the same clues as everyone else. This does not preclude a certain level of intellectual formation, but it is not the intense field of specialization necessary to be considered an "authority" on something.

However – myself and others of similar vocational curiosity, in our attempts to construct this cohesive, rational order, will often revert to the "experts." This is where Xavier Lacosta comes in.

Xavier Lacosta is the journalist responsible for the editorial page article now under discussion. Its length and factual minutiae would suggest his having spent a great deal of time studying the Palestinian question, so much so that he'd have to be given some degree of expert status. When one such as myself has expressed some clearly stated opinions on the same subject, how these opinions match up with those of the "expert" becomes a logical question. Were the factual assertions of the layman (me) correct, and were his interpretations of the facts within reason?

Now, even an "expert," for all his or her detailed research on a particular subject, can have a point of view or preconceived notion that might alter, in varying degrees, the veracity of their postulations. Everyone sees the world through a different set of emotional glasses. When one can sift through the data and find high levels of corroboration, the idea that a concept or interpretation is "correct" begins to take on meaning. All the major historical facts and their interpretations that both myself and Mr. Lacosta touch upon in our respective works, show a goose-stepping synchronization. I'd like to give the reader a few examples:

As the title of Mr. Lacosta's article suggests, its purpose is to debunk many of the myths with which the creation of Israel was based upon.

I quote, "Amongst these justification myths is the idea that the Jews were always in Palestine. This is false. To suggest such a thing would deny the great Dispersion, or expatriation of the Jews in the first century. (–) One of the most evident proofs of this is that only the Moslems confronted the Crusades. There is no narrative that speaks of Jewish troops nor Hebrew leaders or strongmen. (–) The reality is, yes, there were Jews in Palestine of Sephardic or eastern origin, but in very low and insignificant numbers."

OK, here is an important excerpt from my essay "Israelis and Palestinians":

"But if we examine the history of the region since the times of Herod's Roman hegemony and Jesus Christ's non-orgasmic birth, we see the Jews in Palestine reduced to a smattering of people –" (–)

"The first great trauma of the Jewish people was the dispersion of their culture by the Romans. (–) Corroborating this is the fact that the Crusades of medieval times were a purely Christian-Moslem affair. The Jews, basically gone from the region, were not players in this joust."

Lacosta goes on to say:

"Another myth is that, according to the preaching of Theodore Herzl, the Jews scattered about the world had a right to create a state in Palestine after 2,000 years of exile. False. Such kind of legal precedent is not formulated anywhere for anybody."

Here is another excerpt from the essay "Israelis and Palestinians":

"For the last 1,000 years, Palestine has been overwhelmingly imprinted with the Islamic-Arab culture, notwithstanding the drips and blips of Christians, Jews, Copts, Druids or whatever other spiritual dementia the human imagination gives forth with. One predicating the creation of a Jewish state in this region on this historic set of circumstances, might, I suppose, also clamor for the return of North America to the Indians."

Later in his article Lacosta says:

" – the recently arrived Jews were a professional elite with a much higher intellectual level than the Palestinians. This is true because these recently arrived immigrants were from the west. (–) What is almost never mentioned is the overwhelming scorn with which the Jewish immigrants treated the native residents –

Once again, here is the correspondent excerpt from "Israelis and Palestinians":

"It must be reiterated that the vast bulk of the Israeli population are émigrés from developed countries and they have treated the third world natives of Palestine with the same derision and conceit that all colonial powers have shown all through history. But this does not make such behavior acceptable."

These are the themes both myself and Mr. Lacosta coincide in and, as can be seen, there is a good deal of harmony. My essay then goes on to discuss some of the dubious decisions made by ensuing Israeli governments, while his article stays within the bounds of the "myths" used to justify the creation of the Jewish state. This includes a whole host of topics my lack of expertise would preclude me from discussing. This means my acceptance of his facts and interpretations cannot be based upon the kind of "corroboration" demonstrated on previous issues. This means the laymen (me) is flying somewhat blind here and Mr. Lacosta is going to have to convince the layman of his objectivity, regardless of his expert status.

I've now had the opportunity to fully digest the article as an integral whole, and it might be said that Xavier Lacosta has an anti-Israeli-Zionist stance that might be seen as excessive. Some of his assertions and interpretations – including the obligatory reference to the Rothschild family every time the Jews are supposedly up to something in the world – seem forced and contrived. Before getting to them, let's also state that my Jewish bloodline could be clouding my objectivity as well. Where exactly does the truth lie, and how do we find that truth?

Mr. Lacosta, in order to further emphasize the poor treatment doled out by Jewish émigrés to the indigenous population, says that, "it is revealing to note that a number of English colonial officials such as Lawrence and (a few others he mentions) felt profoundly attracted to Islam, while there are no cases of any immigrant Jew having such admiration." For such a statement to be meaningful, one would have to believe that any member of an émigré group trying to claim a land occupied by Moslems for themselves, would be likely to have such feelings. What would make Mr. Lacosta believe that a Jew, or anyone else in a similar historical circumstance, would ever be prone to cultivate such admiration? In addition, from what research source did this assumption come from? The inclusion of such a statement shows an exaggerated, even absurd attempt to make the Jews look bad.

In November of 1947, the United Nations laid out its official plan for the partition of Palestine. As most of us know, it was not accepted by the Arabs. Once the Israeli state formally came into being in May of 1948, the Arabs attacked Israel. This is generally accepted, in the west, as the aggressor act.

Lacosta claims it is just the opposite. He lays out a history of well-organized Jewish terrorist groups operating in the years immediately before independence that assassinated British soldiers and policemen, and constantly harassed and threatened Palestinians into fleeing their homes. He claims Jewish terrorists invaded many Palestinian cities – Jaffa, Haifa, Tiberia, etc. – months before independence. This is his way of stating the Jews attacked the Arabs, and not the other way around.

I find these assertions acceptable, if not airtight. But then he does a peculiar thing. He claims this Jewish terrorism was supported by that loveable, cuddly figure in history, Joseph Stalin. It is hard to find a motive for such help and Lacosta gives none, nor does he offer any clues as to the quantity of such support. Maybe there is some connection between Stalin and the historical acts just discussed, but it seems an almost torturous attempt to link the Jews to a notorious villain of our times, an attempt somewhat out of proportion to whomever else was helping the Jews, who he does not mention (except for the obligatory Rothschild reference).

There is no need to further discuss more detail from the article in question. In trying to calibrate the sincerity or objectivity of an opinion piece, it is not just a question of fact, but of feel, tone, intuition. Mr. Lacosta has given me enough evidence to doubt the purity of his sentiments. The fact that his own prejudices, be they conscious or not, are interfering with his perceptions of reality is not out of the question.

In spite of all that, I do believe his version of this history is much closer to the bull's eye than both the Jewish and official versions in the United States, which are pretty much the same thing. I come to this conclusion by looking back at my early Jewish-American perceptions of these events, and how I came to have them.

American post-war Jewry found a "Bible" for its interpretation of the events in Palestine in a lengthy, "schmaltzy" novel called "Exodus," by Leon Uris. It hit its stride in the late 1950's and was a rotund success, so much so it was made into a blockbuster Hollywood movie with a cast of thousands, a red carpet extravaganza of DeMillean proportions. (It was the kind of film Alec Guinness always showed up in, though I can only remember Eva Marie Saint and Sal Mineo for sure). (My God, Sal Mineo!).

My parents introduced me to "Exodus" when I was about 14 years old, at a time when my life experience was narrowly encased within the confines of the prototypical Jewish-American middle class upbringing. It could have been the first "grown up" novel I ever read, and I do not remember reading another for many years to come. I'm not sure if the fact that I loved it speaks well or poorly for its quality.

In any event, it had its desired effect. I empathized greatly with the "good guys," and found my pride in being Jewish noticeably reinforced. It took me many years of intellectual growth and stimulus encounter to understand that "Exodus" was an extremely ethno-biased, Romantization of history. It took me many years of Moses-like wandering in the huge intellectual desert most human life exists in, before I realized the creation of Israel was less a tear jerking attempt to return a homeland to an aggrieved people, and more a geo-political stunt brokered by Occidental interests, one they now probably wish they'd never thought of.

When I rummage through the attic of my memory and look back upon my "Exodus" experience, what most stands out is not what the book said, but what it failed to say. It is actually incredible to realize that after reading hundreds and hundreds of pages; after having gloried in an epic motion picture, at the time and for many years to come, I had no recollection of the Arabs having anything to do with anything in this whole Homeric saga. Yes, the terrorist history Xavier Lacosta speaks prominently about was an important element of "Exodus" as well, but the fight was always between Jews and British occupational forces. It was as if Palestine was occupied only by Jews and the idea of bringing down colonial rule only pertained to them. Arabs? Didn't they have their own country somewhere else?

Right to this day, the "Exodus" version is still the model for the American concept of this region's history. That is why an article like Lacosta's, in a mainstream media source, always rocks my world.

There is one other thing Mr. Lacosta and myself coincide in: neither of us offer any solutions to this mess.

THE CRASH OF '08

(12/08)

As I write, with the exception of the upcoming game between the Gators and the Crimson Tide, the big story running amuck in our lives is the financial meltdown of 2008, which seems to have been the result of lax oversight – or perhaps it would be better to say the encouragement of a Wall Street scam where people who dress well, smell good, and are adept at folding the New York Times, were trying to make millions of dollars without having a product to sell. If we translate this to English, we get "smoke and mirrors."

I do believe the lead off hitter in the eventual fall of this house of cards was the giant bubble known as AIG. God knows (I doubt it) what a company like this does-did, but there is one thing I do know: those guys had some very cool commercials. There was one in particular that continues to stay with me. A boy of perhaps 10 years wanders into his parents' bedroom in the middle of the night. They awake, turn over and look at him in a blur of semi-consciousness. The boy then delivers a 30 second harangue as to how he is worried about the family's future, its financial strategy, its blend of annuities and IRA's and 401k's, with all the specialized jargon and lingo – just beautiful. At the end of it, the father looks at his worried son and says, "but we have AIG." The boy is immediately relieved, says "oh," and goes back to bed. One watches a commercial like that and thinks, gee, AIG, they really know what they're doing.

A week later they had vaporized.

What started in America, and probably because of Americans and their way of playing the "game," soon spread to the rest of the interconnected global economy. And now you turn on the TV, or read the blogs, and the gloom and doom is so thick and inky, it's like it's never daytime anymore. And every "Situation Room," and every Rachel Maddow, and everything "fair and balanced," and the "most respected names in news," and everything having to do with "information," is overrun with financial experts trying to explain this mountain of poop. If the expert is American, he generally has a name like Morgan Wharton and is a fellow at the Cato or Brookings Institute, so called "think tanks," which leads one to ask, "what have they been thinking"!? If he is English, he has a name like Nigel Brown and is an economic expert at the Financial Times (aren't they all?), and you could just die for his Derby Day accent. Morgan and Nigel will return later in this essay.

Yesterday, I turned on the TV and the big news was that we were officially in a "recession" (someone said it). Not only that, we've been in it for a whole year! And I thought, my God, how did I miss it? It's like, I haven't felt any different, I'm still regular –

and then it hit me: I've been living in a "recession" my whole life. Is that all you've got?

And then I saw one of my favorite experts, the gnome-like Robert Reich, ex-Labor Secretary for Bill Clinton. I love Robert Reich, he's such an articulate little troll. Regardless of what I can understand, he says it so lyrically that I'm ready to follow him anywhere. He's a regular on Big Media TV and the other day he started throwing around the "D" word – like in Studs Terkel and long gray lines of men in moth eaten clothes. And I said to myself, Jerry, it's time to get smart. Why not invest in soup and apples?

Trying to decide if we are in a "recession" or not, or in a "D" (shhh), is something like trying to decide which team is # 1 in college football: there's a lot of data, lots of criteria, but nobody knows for sure. In fact, this ambiguous quality is the basic personality trait of "economics" in general. There seems to be as many theories as to why this happened and how to fix it, as there are "economists." The eventual return of Morgan and Nigel will further focus this idea.

So if the doctors themselves can't seem to find a way to diagnose and cure this economic sickness, how are we, the Monday Night Football Yokels, supposed to understand it? Maybe the key is in not trying to delve deeper and deeper into the ailment. Maybe the key lies in seeing the obvious, in staying simple, in not complicating things. The first thing that strikes me in doing such is the numbers themselves. They seem to be mythical.

By now, we've all been conditioned to the fact that some financial institutions and industries are "too big to fail," and it ain't the fruit and vegetable stand on the corner. Except for a few Republican oligarchs who always have plenty of money, people who feel poverty is neither their fault nor concern, there is a broad consensus here and within the context of the economic game now in use, maybe they are right. So the cavalry is dispatched to rescue these institutions with a sack full of $800 billion of taxpayer money. But as the tide of sewage let loose by this crack in the financial pipes continues to rise above our ankles and up to our knees, the numbers continue to escalate. We are now entering the realm of trillions.

When you round numbers off and simply say so and so millions or billions or trillions, something is lost in the translation. We get used to these words: a billion here, a trillion there, what's for dinner? With this in mind, I am now going to write down an approximate cost that we the government is going to spend on these bailouts, not how many billions or trillions, but a hypothetical exact number: one trillion, four hundred and sixty three billion, seven hundred and forty eight million, six hundred and twenty two thousand, five hundred and eighty three dollars and ninety nine cents (like the gas stations do, just to make it seem cheaper).

And you thought those human size checks they present to Tiger Woods after a tournament were just for show.

OK, now I am going to write this number out with Arabic numerals (and you thought the Arabs were so stupid) and then I am going to write another figure right under it.

$1,463,748,622,583.99

$678

If you have a pulse, you should be wondering what that second number stands for. It is what tens of millions of us make, more or less, after working a full week. I think we can agree, the relationship of these two numbers is in galaxies far, far away.

We live in a society that ranks our worth as human beings very compatibly to the amount of money we have. Given the amount of money represented in the top number – and given the amount of money represented in the bottom number – and given the fact that this money actually exists, I'd say almost all of us have the status of a maggot. In scrutinizing these two numbers, one gets the feeling that almost all of us have none of it, and almost nobody has all of it.

There is an absurd, fraudulent quality to all this. It seems to be fiction more than non-fiction.

And it gets even more absurd.

If we stick to the program and do not get mired in the endless maze of complex economic theories (smokescreens?), and we keep it simple and commonsensical, the next question has to be, "where is all this money coming from"?

Another thing we have been conditioned to in the last 20 years or so is that there is just no money for anything. We've got to cut spending, get more efficient, stop government waste, look out for all those "earmarks," cut the "pork," there's just no money for anything. We have to cut Medicare, it's only a broken leg, get used to it. And for those 40 to 50 million of you who have no health insurance (this number is real), our advice is that you not get sick, we can't afford it. And public libraries, c'mon, who needs libraries, nobody reads anymore anyway, and once we get rid of pre-school and day care, we'll have even less people reading, so give us a break, we just don't have the money. And think about it, do we really need those art and music classes, I mean, did Leonardo Da Vinci ever go to an art class? And those school lunches and breakfasts, get real, you can go buy a chicken sandwich at the Burger Shlurger for 99 cents, if you can't afford that, you deserve to go hungry. And those jobs down at the county that had existed for generations – look, when there's no money, what can we do? Our public parks and recreation facilities, they've been taken over by homeless people anyway, so why spend money on that? And those senior citizen crossing guards at our schools, picking up some extra change working 10 hours a week, in addition to feeling useful and relevant, do we really need them? Kids these days are smart, they know how to cross the street. I know, it's tough, we are all going to have to do our part, suck it up, play like a man, put our pants on one leg at a time and face the grim reality of these difficult times with a smile on our faces and a spring in our steps, because that is what Americans do. And I'm sorry, Mr. and Mrs. America, if all we can do at the moment is lay you off, provide a soup kitchen or two, fight the war in Iraq because it is better to be poor than not free, and bailout AIG and the rest of them with one trillion, four hundred and sixty three billion, seven hundred and forty eight million, six hundred and twenty two thousand, five hundred and eighty three dollars and ninety nine cents, because we just don't have the money.

Upon hearing such a figure, anyone with the IQ of a gibbon, should be asking two questions: 1) how much does it cost to feed a kid a decent meal in school, and, with all due respect to the Redundancy Gods, 2) where is all this money coming from?

Now, the smart money would be betting we are borrowing the money. If you are still paying attention, you might now ask, "who in their right mind would lend that kind of money to an entity as thoroughly bankrupt as the United States"? Well, we have collateral; it's a big country, lots of resources, infrastructure, universities, etc., and the Chinese – the Chinese? You mean that backwards, totalitarian country filled with unhappy people yearning to be free, are going to lend us, the richest, happiest country on Earth, hundreds of billions of dollars? That's right. And if we default, the Chinese get to own the New York Yankees?

And now we are going to bring back Morgan and Nigel, our aforementioned financial experts, and we are going to get in front of the TV as they explain to us why the snide insinuations made in this essay as to the irrational, preposterous nature of their precious economic system are not true, this is how it has to be, and we'll all be better off for it, just shut up and listen.

And here they go: "It is imperative to realize that the annual rate of inflation was putting a tremendous burden on our fiduciary responsibilities in the asparagus market, and once the annuities became due on the roll over of bi-annual interest rates, the situation became untenable in the Straits of Malacca, where piracy was hindering the free flow of credit, but now the balance of payments can ease their way back to normalcy with the help of the Fed, who will keep the price of a good pinot grigio at affordable levels until venture capital is once again ready to prime the sub-mortgage market with a lifeline to our most essential industries – porno, Las Vegas – which will then stimulate the labor market with an electric cattle prod, until everyone can finally go out and buy a new TV."

And it's like we are sitting in a high school algebra class and we've just got the hang of equilateral triangles, but the blackboard is covered with Einstein-like physics equations. And when Morgan and Nigel are done, we'll sit there dumbfounded, scratching our heads, not daring to look at each other, until somebody finally says, "turn on the football game."

And that'll be it. And we will go on being maggots.

THE HOLY ECONOMIC SYSTEM

(3/09)

For this chicken soup philosopher, the main event in the world he lives in becomes the most likely fodder for material. As I write, the sky is falling. Our socio-economic team has blown a 10 run lead in the 9th inning and has brought in its touted young closer, Barack Obama, to save the game.

I've written a lot about the economy lately. Until Brittany Spears does something we can laugh at again (hey, there's good money in being laughed at), the "economy" seems to be the only game in town. Ergo, here we go again.

In order to do so, I will eventually bring back our fictional financial "experts," Morgan Wharton and Nigel Brown, in representation of all such creatures (see essay, "The Crash of '08"). Morgan is a "scholar" at one of those Cato-Brookings type "think tanks," a peculiar name for institutions that seem to have little relevance to either word. Nigel is a financial expert at London's "Financial Times," where even the Jamaican lady who cleans his office is a financial expert. But first, some background:

When I work, I listen to a goodly amount of egghead news and commentary on National Public Radio. Except for some specialized publications and outer reaches of the Blogosphere, NPR is about as "egghead" as America gets –

and it ain't nothing to write home about. Much like all of Big Media, the economy, economy, economy, – the economy. Since the Holy Economic System fell into its "Chernobyl" mode, I've been subjected to a lot of roundtables, interviews with experts, debates amongst partisans, G20 summits, on and on, from the eggheads and commercial news alike. It all sounds very much the same wherever you are on the viewing-listening dial. What seems to separate the eggheads from the Wolf Blitzer crowd, is that the eggheads do a lot less Alex Rodriquez. But the message is pretty much the same.

This essay was hatched from 2 in depth discussions of the economy (what else?) I heard on NPR. I cannot remember the names of the participants, nor the organizations they represent, which would be something like knowing who's pitching long relief for the Florida Marlins these days. As a result, I will use Morgan and Nigel to represent these roles, because – really, once you've heard one economist, you've heard them all.

Why do they all sound so alike? Elementary: something like 100% of the economic "experts" we hear from in our culture have been trained and nourished in the current form of neo-liberal capitalism. It is the breast they feed from. They are its advocates, and when it functions poorly – and really, in a global sense, it always functions poorly – they end up being its apologists and rationalizers. They only carry on a debate within the framework of this economic system that has engendered them. This framework could be described as puny in comparison to the abundance of choices humans have in developing and distributing the world's resources.

So there I was one morning, listening to the Diane Ream Show on NPR. This is a program that could fool you for awhile, but in the end, it too is constricted to that narrow framework of acceptability just mentioned above. And Morgan Wharton (or was it Nigel Brown?) was expounding upon a tsunami that has yet to drown the shores of the current economic disaster, that being the amount of personal debt rung up and still outstanding in the United States of Gringoland. In the words of that hip-hop, basketball playing sage, Alan Iverson, "we're talking about plastic, man, plastic." You thwap it down on the counter, they run it through that vaginal-like slot, and voila! you can now go home with those $200 shoes you just "had to have." (See essay, "Destructive People").

Morgan is very worried about this. According to him, the amount of personal debt still outstanding in the United States is equal to 100% of the Gross National Product. The last time this happened was in – let's look it up, one moment – oh, yeah, in 1929.

Ahh, the memories –

Very interesting, but here is where Morgan begins to play the apologist role for "his" economic system. He starts blubbering away on how it really isn't a question of regulation or non-regulation, of government action or inaction, of privatization or nationalization, of stimulating or letting it be – no. It's a question of personal responsibility, of each and every one of us not being reckless with our fiscal possibilities. We've been living beyond our means. It's not really the system, it's us. Personal responsibility.

That is a lot of personal bull.

Sure, in the grand stew of human endeavor, there might be a teaspoon of truth in Morgan's assertion, but it is overwhelmed by not only what our economic system leads us to do, but, even more importantly, what it <u>needs</u> us to do.

One of the milestone moments in human history was the invention of the television. It is unfortunate this wonderful apparatus has been set into our culture in the way it has. TV has become the salesman of consumerism, acting with robotic persistence in making us want the things that nourish the Holy Economic System. As if that weren't enough, Morgan and his ilk decided to pile on by propagating the universal use of the credit card. This was no accident. This was a calculated effort to make it as easy as possible for any consumer whim to be consummated. Which begs the question – who gave everybody these credit cards? Hey, Morgan, if we are talking about responsibility here, maybe this is where we should look first. After all, it was the "experts" that did this.

So talking about "personal responsibility" in such a socio-economic environment is a hollow rationalization for the poop that's been piling up. But it is just pocket change compared to the real problem. What Morgan seems to ignore is that his Holy Economic System cannot work unless the mass of people are actually living on the edge of their credit cards. The amount of consumption necessary to sustain it is preposterous. If the personal responsibility referred to by Morgan actually happened, the Holy Economic System becomes sick. It cannot sustain its work force. In such a system, the idea of personal responsibility is turned on its head: we must spend – not be frugal and responsible.

About a week later, on the same Diane Ream Show, I heard an even more absurd apology for the Holy Economic System. About a half hour into her show, Diane will say, "and now, let's open the phones for our listeners – " All programs with listener participation have "screeners" who maintain each show's particular brand of PTA-Kiwanis Club approval for questions. In addition, the 7-second delay serves as the final firewall for poor taste. In this instance, perhaps they let one get away, and it could be the best question I've ever heard on such a show.

"Tell me Diane, why is it, when you talk about anything having to do with the economy, you never have anyone on who is opposed to this economic system? Why is it always people from within the system, the same organizations, the same type of experts? Why don't you ever include someone who doesn't like this system, instead of people who are just trying to put it back together"?

Have you ever been in a group where someone has farted and there are those prolonged, awkward moments, where everyone is trying to ignore it and act normally – Me? You? Who?

This question was the fart in the Diane Ream Show, and an awkward silence in radio is about the same as the cable going out in television. Diane tried to rescue her show, "but – well – they are the experts – I don't know – who else could I – " At this point, Nigel Brown (or was it Morgan Wharton?) came to the rescue. Firmly, confidently, "look, in spite of its shortcomings, free market capitalism has still been shown to be the most efficient and fair way to distribute goods and services."

Enough of this insurrection! Next question.

I'd like to have a nickel for every time somebody defending the status quo has said, "yeah, but it is still – " "Yeah, slavery, for all its badda-boom, it is still – " or, "yeah, women not voting, it might be yadda-yadda, but it is still – " or, "not letting workers organize could be seen as blah-blah, but it is still – " or, "segregation might be seen as dippity-doo, but it is still – " Here's a philosophical rule of thumb: anytime someone defending the status quo says "it is still" or any derivative thereof, change what is being defended as quickly as possible.

Nigel claims his neo-liberal capitalism is efficient. On a scale of 1 to 10, 10 being perfect efficiency, the Holy Economic System gets a 0. It wastes more resources than anyone could have conceived of perhaps no more than 50 years ago. The next time you buy a 2-inch plastic car for junior to play with, see where it was made. That's right, 10,000 miles of shipping just to make that insignificant item **cheaper** (see essay, "Walmart or The Stupid Economy"). The Holy Economic System is so wasteful, so destructive, so ecologically irresponsible, we'd have to invent another word for the inefficiency it entails.

And here's another good one; Nigel thinks the Holy Economic System is fair. My guess is that Nigel lives on planet Earth, but maybe he's never heard of Bangladesh, or seen what is happening on the Mexican-American border, or made aware of the waves of Africans on less than seaworthy boats washing ashore in the Canary

Islands. There is a majority of dirt-poor people out there, and they are a part of Nigel's Holy Economic System too.

The public discourse in America has been strangling in its own rhetoric for way too long. The problem is that only 2 choices are given for socio-economic policy: free market capitalism or Stalinist communism. In the simple-minded terms of Yankee propaganda, the latter lost. That leaves just one choice. This is like letting a pitcher throw only 75 MPH fastballs, and right down the middle. Hopefully, our touted young reliever, Barack Obama, has more pitches than that.

Relevant Material:

"You will never have enough of what you don't need."

When asked what we should acquire in lieu of material things, she answered, "experiences."

These two remarks are from April Lane Benson, a renowned psychologist specializing in compulsive buying.

"SAVING" AT WALMART

(11/09)

Anyone using their visual capacities to stare at a television in America these days will soon realize that the beast of retail has been inundating the airwaves with its latest advertising campaign. Walmart's clout in the world is so gargantuan, it almost naturally invites both suspicion and resentment as to how it has cornered such a huge percentage of the world's consumptive habit. This suspicion has spawned a whole host of negative studies detailing the unsavory aspects of its corporate personality, including its less than admirable labor practices, its "Big Box" invasion of small town America which has left the urban cores of so many picturesque places dead or barely breathing, amongst other things. This has put Walmart in a perpetual public relations battle in defense of its solid citizen corporate reputation. Its primary defense is that, "yeah, yeah, yeah, blah, blah, blah, we've heard it all before, but the bottom line is that we sell everything cheaper, so rotate on that."

This has proven very effective, and its latest advertising blitz plays heavily upon this theme, perhaps more than ever. We'll get back to this later.

(Just as an aside, the town where I live has a decent cross section of corporate retail outlets, including Sears, K-Mart, CVS, Walgreen's, Home Depot, Office Max, Radio

Shack, Ross, Champ's, yadda-yadda. There is no Walmart. And yet, the bombardment of Walmart television advertising could be compared to what England endured in WWII, while the outlets actually doing business here seem to have no or little air force at all. What this says about the omnipotence of Walmart's commercial power is unclear to me, but I'll let the reader chew it over anyway.)

The art of lying, in the socio-economic system currently pinning the world to the mat, has reached its most sublime levels ever (see essays "The Demoralized Zone" and "Industrial Size Lying," amongst others). The competitive persuasion needed to win over a consumer has created a marketing industry far larger than the industrial mechanisms needed to produce the products. It is not the job of this industry to tell the truth. At times, the truth and the persuasion coincide, but that is totally coincidental and not relevant. The persuasion is the only thing relevant.

The best kinds of lies are ones where nothing untrue has actually been spoken. This kind of lie will focus on a very constricted space of reality and say something obviously true within the confines of this limited space. This narrow little truth – a "little white truth," if you will – is used as a diversion or smokescreen meant to focus one's attention away from the Big Lie the liar wants to go unnoticed. The consumer who is the target of such tactics only has direct access to the narrow little space where the little white truth is penned up. The only data available to this consumer corroborates what the advertiser is saying. But it ignores a much wider range of factors this consumer has no access to, or, due to its complexity, has neither the time nor intellect to unravel. Once unraveled, the little white truth becomes a big, fat lie.

I will now try to unravel it.

Walmart's latest Pavlovian exercise in mind control is an excellent example of this. Obviously, in its perpetual public relations battles against those criticizing its business practices, the low cost to the consumer has been its most powerful weapon of justification. Its latest round of advertising makes cost its **only** justification. This is where they've decided to dig in. This is their Maginot Line. Nobody will ever pierce this low cost entrenchment.

These new commercials, after a more general trumpeting of this low cost persona, claims the average family can save $3,000 a year shopping at Walmart. How such a figure is arrived to as well as its veracity, is always *k-ching* for thought, but let's give our upstanding corporate citizen the benefit of the doubt. At the very least, we can all agree Walmart does sell cheaper than others, so –

– within this narrow terrain of operations, that being retail cost, the advertiser has spoken no falsehoods.

But there is a much wider range of factors to take into account. Walmart is only showing us the bright side of the moon. It wants us to not only forget the dark side, but to not even acknowledge it has ever existed. If the dark side actually did not exist, the moon would lose its equilibrium and spiral out of control. The same would happen to Walmart if its dark side, the side they do not want us to know about, did not exist.

What is this dark side, the side that keeps planet Walmart in orbit, which makes it function in such a profitable way?

When one talks about "savings," retail cost is only one side of the coin. The other side is purchasing power; how much money do I have to spend? What percentage of my income is being used to buy the mundane things I buy at Walmart? How much is left for other things or savings? Over the last 25 years or so, the time frame where Walmart has conquered the world and the current form of neo-liberal, "savage capitalism" has put the world in a headlock that has brought it to the brink of disaster, to claim income has kept up with prices, even in Walmart, would be a very hard sell. This is especially true amongst the average Walmart shopper who works for a living, earns a wage, gets a salary, sits in the bleachers at Wrigley Field, and did not invest with Bernie Madoff (Walmart is one of the demographic centers of "average").

If, over this quarter century of personal fiscal struggle, the $3,000 Walmart claims to save you annually is offset by a $4,000 loss in purchasing power – do the math. (These figures are hypothetical, but make the point).

"But gee, we'd be even worse off without them. Can we blame Walmart for this?"

Quite frankly, the answer is yes.

Walmart is not only the world's biggest retail business, the last I heard, it was the world's biggest corporation! To think a business enterprise of these dimensions could be a benign force in how the world functions would be something like believing the world is flat. Walmart has been a trendsetter in developing the kind of capitalism now operating globally. Although there are some commendable aspects of its business model that do lower costs for everyone – primarily its distribution systems – this is not the foundation of its success. That resides in a third world labor force, a labor pool not employed by Walmart (what, me worry?), that makes almost every product you buy in the "Big Box" (see essay "Walmart or The Stupid Economy"). It is a labor pool earning a wage an average American family would have trouble living on for hours, let alone provide a decent living. It is a business model that has sucked good paying manufacturing jobs out of the "homeland." It has made an end run around unions and more or less defeated them. Its own employees are used in such a way that many benefits that used to accompany such work have been erased from the blackboard. Undoubtedly, other corporate retailers are or will begin to emulate this business model pioneered by Walmart. This has a ripple effect through the global economy that depresses wages in the developed world as well. It is ironic –

– that Ronald Reagan, one of the original heroes of this economic model, asked, in getting himself elected, what is the proper question to ask right now, "Are you better off now than 4 years ago?" All Walmart consumers should be asking themselves if they are better off now than before the days of Walmart. For most of these consumers, the answer would probably be no.

The little white truth becomes a big, fat lie.

ST. RONALD OF HOLLWOOD

(10/12)

"St. Ronald of Hollywood" has appeared before in these pages (see essays "Poliomyelitis," "The Chinese Advantage" and others). The moment has arrived to further expound upon a figure in American history whose Deification is perhaps the least connected to the reality of Earthly outcome than any other American politician. Ronald Reagan, with the help of his Hollywood apprenticeship in front of a camera, sold 2 basic premises to the American people that have retarded our well being for almost a half century now. Later in this essay I will expose these 2 bogus premises, but before doing so I'd like to flip the flapjack on one of his most successful political utterances by asking the following:

"Do you think we are better off now as a nation than we were when Reagan became President"?

The pinpoint of the American economic pyramid Ronald Reagan most represented <u>is</u> better off – let's use the in vogue nomenclature of the 1% to describe that segment of America – but even a pre-Alzheimer's Ronald Reagan, if he could summon up a minimal amount of objectivity, would have to agree the majority of us have either tread water, begun to sink, or drowned since. Undoubtedly, he'd attribute this to not staying the course of his policies enough, but an in depth reality check reveals that we have stayed that course way too closely.

Put simply, St. Ronald, for whom schools, highways and airports have been named – my God, it has even been suggested he go up on Mt. Rushmore – is a **FRAUD**.

The seed for this essay began while watching the American collapse in golf's Ryder Cup. There was a time when the mere thought of an American athletic conglomerate falling in such an ignominious way, as well as the thought of a bunch of foreigners actually remounting such an American advantage, would be unthinkable. Obviously, linking a country's athletic prowess to its generic well-being could almost be considered a ridiculous exercise. The Soviet Union maintained a formidable athletic juggernaut at a time when it was entering a moribund decline into dismantlement. Such highly successful nations as England, Japan or France, rarely protagonize leadership in the athletic world. But it might also be asked if any cultural manifestation is <u>totally</u> irrelevant. I'm certainly not about to link this year's disastrous Ryder Cup performance to any precipitous decline in the American *"zeitgeist."* The United States of America is still the world's largest economy, still the world's foremost military power, and still a cultural giant with much appeal. But – have we begun to lose our "swagger"?

Athletes understand the concept of "intimidation." Quite frequently, someone's success can create an aura of invincibility that can keep one at the top a bit longer than his or her waning athletic ability should. Has the American nation begun to lose its aura of intimidation, not just in an athletic sense, but in our long admired ability to innovate? Have we lost our quasi-monopoly on vanguard-like technological development? Does the rest of the world now look our way and think they can do it as well or better? Even worse, do they look our way and think they don't want to copy that? Have we begun to stagnate, to rest on our laurels? Have we begun to buy our own narrative (propaganda?) to such an extent that we've become complacent?

Certainly, there is no definitive answer to any of the questions just asked above, but it would also be dishonest to not find some element of "yes" in play. In spite of the heretical nature inherent in criticizing St. Ronald, I'll say the following anyway: that element of "yes" can be attributed to the kind of mindset Ronald Reagan left this nation mired in. This mindset is embodied in the 2 premises spoken of at the outset of this essay, 2 premises that Reagan planted, watered, fertilized and nurtured into full grown trees with deep roots.

1) Government can't do anything, "it is not the answer, it is the problem." 2) If your life is not what you want it to be, it is because you are being cheated from <u>below</u>, by "welfare queens" and freeloaders living off your hard earned money.

These 2 premises – and oh, by the way, neither of which is remotely true – have changed the course of American politics. They have retarded our emotional growth as a nation and are the primary legacies of a President whose canonization is as much an act of propaganda as the 2 premises themselves are.

The first premise has allowed the private sector to run through our culture like a rabid dog off its leash. It has created a psychotic financial sector that has become more adept at paper pushing shell games than at investing in productive business enterprises. With government staying out of it (hey, it's the problem, right?), some of the most immense fortunes in American history have been made by people who have not developed, produced or maintained a product; by people who have not provided employment for others; by people who have not done anything to create the kind of private enterprise that benefits the society in general (hmmm – Mitt Romney). The government staying out of it has allowed the upper echelons of the private sector to make more money without getting better and without sharing it reasonably with the rest of us who provide the working foundation for the 1%'s well being. By not letting this working foundation of people in on a reasonable share of the booty, our economy has not only been weakened, but even more importantly, it has retarded our evolution as a nation.

A logical result of this mindset is that the government has no role to play in shaping and developing the common good. The most egregious result of this kind of Reaganesque thinking is America's Neanderthal way of dealing with corporal illness. Its mechanisms for delivering medical attention can almost be described as a laughing stock throughout the world. Believing that "government is the problem" has weakened public education and made access to higher education more and more difficult for more people. The same can be said for a whole host of Social Contract ideas that provide more social mobility and opportunity. This is not an adequate space to be more specific, but anyone being quasi-honest with themselves cannot suggest our country has improved in these areas since St. Ronald of Hollywood polluted our minds.

One of the great myths attached to the "government is the problem" voodoo is that the private sector can always do it better. Over the years, I've paid particular attention to this assertion in an attempt to verify its message. As I sit here writing in the here and now, I can say with some confidence there is no empirical evidence for this. To compare the role of government to the private sector is a primal error in itself. The 2 things do not exist for the same reasons. Their goals are different. For a businessperson to claim he or she is more suited to govern is ludicrous. Being a businessperson is an important but finite task in our culture, just as being an engineer, doctor, soldier or entertainer is. Being able to enrich your stockholders is no proof one can govern better for the country as a whole.

Does this mean the public sector is inherently better? No, of course not. The task before us is to find out which tasks are best suited for public or private sector action and to delegate these tasks properly. There should be no propensity to believe more in one or the other, there should only be a search for proper usage. This is the only way a modern nation-state can move forward. Ronald Reagan convinced us to abandon this course. This is what is known as a big mistake. There are many countries in the developed world that, rather than abandon this course, have further developed it. Their living standards and technological innovation are now on a par or have surpassed us.

In the end, both the private and public sectors rely on human beings to carry out their missions. How this manpower is mustered, delegated and led is the prime ingredient for success, not whether it is the private or public sector that is doing it.

2) The second concept, that is, you are getting cheated from below, is more a political stunt than a sincerely felt position. When Reagan first convinced the nation to believe this, it resulted in a block of voters known as the "Reagan Democrats." This block of voters, to some extent, is still intact. It is a fairly homogenous galvanization of white working males in the bottom half of America's economic landscape. They can be easily led into scapegoating "niggas," "spics," "wetbacks" and such for whatever their own hard work does not provide them. They are the group of Americans who most consistently vote against their own interests by voting Republican. Their discontent has been deflected in the wrong direction, while they vote for those who deny them their just piece of the American pie. This is not just manifested in the decreasing purchasing power of their wages, but in the persistent, stubborn dismantlement of the Social Contract Ronald Reagan put in motion. This has hindered the ability of their children to climb the ladder of the American Dream. Ronald Reagan preyed upon the psychological insecurity of wage earners looking for some way to rationalize their humble status in our society. He got them to look away from their true enemies, that is, a

financial oligarchy that continues to take more for them and give less to them.

It can be safely said that whenever there are public assistance programs, or unemployment benefits, or public subsidies or grants or scholarships and such, there will be some people jobbing the system and getting something they don't deserve. But it is a minor annoyance rather than a major snafu, a minor annoyance St. Ronald of Hollywood used to allow the people he really represented to job the system to the tune of hundreds of billions of dollars. If we don't include Medicare and Social Security, 2 Social Contract programs that have proven highly successful and relatively easy to pay for if our collective wealth as a nation were used properly, the costs for the rest of these assistance programs are truly a fly on the back of the elephant that is the budget of the United States of America. Such expenditures have never even remotely had anything to do with whatever grievances a Reagan Democrat would have.

Ronald Reagan was a turning point in American history, one that turned us in the wrong direction. I'd rather see Pee Wee Herman on Mt. Rushmore than Ronald Reagan.

Relevant Material: I heard an interesting statistic on TV the other day. The government's annual contribution to Public Broadcasting is about the same as it costs to keep one soldier in Afghanistan for a week.

GUNS

(4/13)

Guns.

Columbine, Aurora, Newtown, amongst many others, as well as the death toll taken on a daily basis within the confines of the world's most advanced nation (as they tell us here in the good 'ol US of A) –

Guns. We're talking a lot about guns lately. Perhaps it is a stain on our national legacy to say we've finally begun to think seriously about this insane proliferation of firearms only after 20 little children had to succumb to it, snuffed out, gone, dead, in a matter of seconds, beautiful children, perhaps the most telling example of why we are here on this planet; of why we exist. The usual daily carnage of gun violence was not enough to move us. Maybe we should be more ashamed than outraged for this latest outburst of psychotic behavior.

The "gun people" have a lot of assembly line rhetoric for the attitudes they represent. One such piece of excrement is that the rest of us don't understand them or the use of firearms. They say we just don't get it. In my case there is some truth to that. I've never so much as touched a real firearm. Growing up, there were no such things in our homes or any of our relative's homes. We lived free from the paranoia of not being lethally armed. It was not a factor in our lives. Guns were for TV.

But I get it!

I'm not a parent. Although I could never plumb the depths of horror a parent in this situation might feel, I can have some understanding of the despair without borders or time limits a parent losing a young child can feel. I don't have to be a parent to understand that. Perhaps the most heroic political act I've ever seen is being carried out by those grieving Connecticut parents and siblings who refuse to go away. They are like "the ghosts of Christmas past" embedding themselves in the conscience of America. Every time I see them on TV my eyes well up in a liquid haze. Imagine having gone through such a cataclysmic disaster without sitting around feeling sorry for yourself, something none of us would have blamed them for. By now I feel less sorrow than immense admiration for them. If you don't understand that, you can be Wayne LaPierre or Senator Cruz of Texas.

It is almost embarrassing to think we Americans are debating the propriety of weapons with the ability to reel off endless rounds off bullets in seconds in the possession of anyone who might want them. Do we let anyone drive a car or an airplane? Do we let a 3 year old cross a busy street unattended? I consider our gun debate to be no more complicated than the latter question. Anyone not in agreement with that – is mentally ill.

I recently got a ticket for not using my seat belt. When I was leaving the courthouse after paying the fine, I had a lucid moment when I realized that, in this state, my not wearing a seat belt was considered a greater threat to society than a person possessing the kind of weaponry we might see in the Afghan war. So the next time you don't buckle up, just remember what a menace to society you are. Bring your Glock or AK47, but don't forget to fasten your seat belt unless you want the full force of the law to come crashing down on you.

Another entry into the medley of rhetoric from the "gun people" goes like this: no matter what you do to legislate gun control, people with sinister designs will always find a way to do harm.

This statement is not only true, it is so stupid it brings its sincerity into question (the sincerity of those speaking for the "gun people" will soon be raised in this essay). It is something like saying why wear helmets in a football game because people will get injured anyway. Or why give people speeding tickets because there will always be people speeding. Or why send people to prison because there will always be crime. Or, or, or – such a list would be infinite. Or how about this one: why have policemen when we can all have guns. Why have laws at all, or governments, when we can all have guns. (Cue the Beatles) All you need is guns –

One of the most prolific genres in the pantheon of the motion picture industry is the "western" – Gary Cooper westerns, John Wayne westerns, spaghetti westerns, Lee Van Cleef and Eli Wallach, *Gunsmoke*, *Maverick* and tomahawk haircuts. The western has left no one on the planet unfamiliar with the American "wild west." We all remember law west of the Pecos, meaning the lack thereof. Long before the advent of MLB or NBA, of FIFA or the NFL, the "wild west" already had its favorite sport – the gunfight. We're talking about athletes here, playing a sport with very high stakes. Winner take all. There was always some young buck coming along to challenge the fastest draw in the west with guns in holsters worn as naturally as a baseball glove, standard equipment for every man in town. The "wild west."

Nobody living in the 19th century ever saw a western. This widespread form of entertainment is reserved for those of us privy to the technology of the 20th century and beyond. Certainly, one of the fundamental assumptions for those of us who have watched westerns is that we don't live like that anymore. We've moved beyond that, are more civilized. We now have police, judges and the rule of law. Indeed, a theme running through many westerns is to subdue this vigilante gun justice and turn these virgin places into communities we could marry and raise our children in. The fact that we don't live in the "wild west" anymore is looked upon as a sign of emotional progress by all of us.

Almost all.

One listening to the assembly line rhetoric of the "gun people" could easily conclude they see **less** gun proliferation as a sign of decay; as an emotional jump backwards; as a retro-step towards barbarism. Their party line ga-ga could lead us to believe the environment of the "wild west" is the highest form of civilization we have ever developed. Perhaps they watch a western with a teary eyed nostalgia for the "good 'ol days," when everyone walked around with a holster strapped to their hip containing the erect penis of their manhood for all to see – yeah man, that's civilization!

Regardless of the assembly line rhetoric of the "gun people," nobody wants to live in the "wild west" anymore.

And that brings me to Wayne LaPierre, the mouthpiece for the "gun people."

Perhaps some of you are wondering why I have not mentioned the National Rifle Association in this essay. Why have I chosen to say the "gun people"?

The NRA and its membership are not the real protagonists in this struggle. The NRA and its membership are not the ones most responsible for the push back against the civility of no-brainer gun laws. The NRA has now become a front organization for those who sell guns. Wayne LaPierre, in spite of his position as president of the NRA, does not really work for the NRA. He works for those who profit selling guns. He works for financial interests, not gun owners. To continue using the NRA as the boogeyman here deflects blame away from those truly responsible for this idiocy.

Can anything be said in defense of a man like Wayne LaPierre? Aren't there lots of people lobbying for narrow financial interests that do not coincide with the "common good"? Is Wayne LaPierre no different than the person shilling for Goldman-Sachs?

Put yourself in the place of Wayne LaPierre. Think of all the assembly line rhetoric he regurgitates so naturally just to protect the profits of a mega-industry – the 2nd amendment, good guys with guns killing bad guys with guns, arming teachers, opposing the government (guns must be better than votes), ad nauseam. He does not say these things because he religiously believes in the 2nd amendment, or because a housewife with a 30-bullet clip can kill a burglar. No. He says it so an industry can go on making billions of dollars. It's for the money!

But, you might say, lots of people do it "for the money" in the society we live in. True, but Wayne LaPierre does it for the money made over the dead bodies of little children. This is more than just power lunch greed and boardroom shenanigans. This is something that flirts with the word "evil."

Could you do what Wayne LaPierre does?

PART IV

RACE, RELIGION, ETHNICITY, GENDER, THE THINGS THAT DIVIDE US

A RACIST JOKE

It would be difficult for any chicken soup philosopher living in the United States to not touch upon race relations. The United States is a multi-racial society. This means two things: 1) There will be racism, and 2) There will be progress in resolving these problems. Only a culture of such racial-ethnic diversity, a culture where these varying blood lines deal with each other regularly – see each other, work with each other, come in contact with each other's talents, admire each other's "ho," etc. – can ever come to grips with racial-ethnic prejudice. A truly sincere effort in fighting racism took way too long to happen in America, not really beginning until after WWII. But once the ball got rolling, this country has struggled valiantly with this problem, so much so that at least "officially," the United States can be considered a non-racist society. (See essay "Racism").

But let's not be too superficial. Old habits die slowly and there is still much work to do in this context. We are moving in the right direction, but we are dragging some anchors that hold us back. Although I might consider this normal, it would be incorrect to say the problem still does not need to be monitored. Fortunately – and this is an indication of our progress – those who have traditionally been the victims of prejudice are strong enough to not let that happen. But if their guard ever came down, retro-racial attitudes would flow into this void more quickly than we might expect.

Racism still stalks the human condition, even in a place like the United States, which could be considered enlightened in this area.

I recently heard a terribly racist joke. I confess, I laughed and I laughed with gusto. If I must be honest (and I must, it's a problem of mine), I believe all people, deep down in the boiler room-basement of their minds, carry around some racial prejudice. Would I have been as fond of Larry Bird if he was just another black basketball star? But, at least with regard to my own conscience, I am far from being a racist.

OK, although it might not be as effective put to paper, here is the joke: A Chinese guy walks into an all black bar, walks up to the bartender and says, "hey nigger, give me a drink." The bartender is stunned, but instead of getting violent, he says, "Look, I'm going to try and show you something. Let's change places; you become the bartender and I'll be the customer." They change places. The black guy walks up to the bar. "Hey, Chink, give me a drink." The Chinese guy replies, "Sorry, we don't serve niggers here."

Even in thinking about this joke in the most superficial way – that is, without giving it the least intellectual attention – there is something horribly degrading here for an Afro-American. But if we do give it some thought, it gets much worse.

For one thing, the joke is perpetrated by a Chinese person, an ethnic group that was almost considered "semi-human" in this country for many generations, and given the lowly treatment such position would warrant. For an

Afro-American, this further salts the wound of this joke. We can pour it on by mentioning that the black bartender takes an extremely civilized course of action. He tries to educate, to enlighten, to do the right thing ... and he gets humiliated anyway! But even in a broader sense, if one truly scrutinizes the nature of this joke, we might as well take the top off the salt shaker and drop it all in.

Once I began pondering the broader implications of this joke, the first thing I asked myself was if it could be as remotely funny using any other racial or ethnic group as its target? After awhile, I had to sadly admit the answer was "no." The Afro-American experience is so intimately tied to this kind of treatment, they almost go together like a pair of eyes. Certainly, "micks," "kikes," "dagos," "polacks," etc., have all been subject to some form of degradation, but a systematic denial of both public and private services is generally not a deeply rooted part of their identity. Even for the more racially distinguishable 3rd world immigrants of more recent vintage, these barriers have been substantially broken down, mainly due to the stubborn work of the Afro-American. And this is yet another of the sad ironies of the black experience in America: Although no racial-ethnic group other than the almost extinct American Indian can claim greater longevity living here, they still suffer the scars of prejudice more than anyone.

I am Jewish. My guilt in finding the joke so funny was such that I experimented with using my own ethnicity as the brunt of the joke, thus giving me the opportunity to tell it with a clear conscience. When one jokes about oneself, the result is much more acceptable.

It just doesn't work.

Certainly, if I may understate the matter, the Jewish people have had to deal with more than their fair share of ethnic persecution. Persecution is an integral part of the Jewish identity (see essay, "Schindler's List"). But the hatred for the Jew takes on a different personality than the racial prejudice felt by Black America. In general, Jews were never meant to feel inferior or less than human, at least not until the periodic outbursts against them had become reality. Whereas Blacks were despised almost in an evolutionary way, as if they were lesser animals, Jews have been <u>resented</u> (which could even mean some subconscious envy) by those idiotic enough to have such feelings. Their communities were usually prosperous, their children well educated, their culture intact and functioning well. Obviously, the fact that they don't believe in the same God as the ocean of people surrounding them is a good jumping off point for such resentment. When this resentment broke out of its cage, the results were horrifying, but there have never been separate water fountains for Jews, or separate waiting rooms, or bathrooms, nor has any Jew ever had to go to the back of a bus, as if their physical presence was something offensive or distasteful. Jews were playing in the Major Leagues long before anyone ever heard of Jackie Robinson. They've always owned property, they've always been able to vote, nobody has ever bought and sold them.

No, try telling this joke using a Jew or any other ethnic group as its target; you will not get a laugh. Sad but true.

Another question I put to myself was whether I knew any black person intimately enough to tell them the joke. I am friendly with a reasonable amount of black people. I work with a few; I've played tennis over a long period of time with a number of them, etc. I've been a high school basketball referee for more than 20 years, working primarily with Afro-Americans. One develops a very strong bond doing such a thing, at least on the court. And yet, I could not find the confidence to ever dare tell any black man this joke. I've been able to laugh at some Jewish jokes, as I'm sure Italians or Irish or Polish people have been able, to some extent, to accept some of the jokes made at their expense. But for now, this joke still seems way too close to where the bat meets the ball for a black man to feel comfortable with. It's just too much a part of their identity, their history, even their heritage (as is persecution for a Jew), to make light of face to face.

Further compounding my guilt is the fact that I've not only enjoyed this joke but I've told it to others. Does the fact that it is a very funny joke mitigate its offensiveness? No, of course not. Undoubtedly, the joke is funny because there is something very real here, something that actually portrays our culture with some degree of accuracy. If it is painful for a segment of our society, that pain is real, as is the racism underlying the joke's conception. Perhaps the most valuable thing I've learned from this joke is just how real it is. To wit:

The half dozen or so times I've told this joke to others, it has never failed to get a laugh. Most people, like myself, show a bit of guilt, but it doesn't stop them from laughing. But there are also a healthy percentage of folks who show their true colors, who revel in the joke, as if the world has finally been put right. Both the joke teller and those who laughed give them the confidence to open up, as if we were all brothers in racism now. To hell with all this political correctness, godammit, let's call a spade a spade. These people usually have a few racist jokes of their own to tell, or some political gripes – did you hear Jessie Jackson going on again?, etc. – to air out. Surprisingly enough, we are not talking about some "good ol' boy," tailgating rednecks, whooping it up for the Crimson Tide while gnawing on some barbecue. No. These attitudes have surfaced from people you'd have never suspected it from. It's as if you've suddenly found that your respectable next-door neighbor has a massive collection of child-porn in his basement.

In what can only be seen as a remarkable alignment of the heavenly bodies, the Rush Limbaugh story, where he makes some racial remarks about black quarterbacks, hit the airwaves while I was writing this essay. The next essay I write will pertain to this incident and will be titled "Rush Eats Foot." It could be read in conjunction with this one.

RUSH LIMBAUGH'S JESUS

(1/10)

Unfortunately, it is becoming increasingly difficult to ignore the lunacy of America's most prominent neo-fascist, Rush Limbaugh. The scope of his influence in the American "body politique" can no longer be defeated with the haughty disdain of more rational intelligence. Its threat to the sanity of the country (which also means the world in the case of this country) must now be confronted. As a result, he is back in the pages of this ever growing mass of chicken soup philosophy.

I recently saw a blurb from an interview with Limbaugh that centered on health care. Limbaugh would rather be kicked in the balls than live in a country that provided a decent level of medical care for all. His reasoning went something like this: if you have a lot of money, you can have a big, beautiful house. If you don't have a lot of money, you live in an apartment or some lesser structure. Why should it be any different for health care?

Admittedly, I am just paraphrasing here, but I ask the reader to trust me – that was pretty darn close. Now go back and read it again. That is what he said.

This is the man who has become the driving force behind one of our 2 political parties.

The light bulb for this essay went on when I began to think how ironic it was that the most solid base of support for Limbaugh and the right wing of American politics he represents, comes from the fanaticism of the country's most fervent Christians. Universal health care as part of the Social Contract would not only lose amongst this constituency, it would be squashed and obliterated beyond debate. Can anyone out there imagine Jesus Christ voting against universal health care, against healing the sick, whoever they are, whatever they have? **Just what Jesus are these people worshipping?**

In answering that question, I've decided to write a short story called "Rush's Jesus."

RUSH'S JESUS

There is a wonderful public park that runs, like Chile along the west coast of South America, for a few miles along the upper west side of Manhattan. Its most prominent feature is a wide walkway or promenade that is the spine of the park throughout its length. On a nice day, this promenade is bustling with joggers, bikers, skaters, moms and dads with their kids, and just about the whole human burlesque enjoying some unencumbered moments in harmonious fraternity with the world. As one might expect, this promenade is flanked by hundreds of comfortable benches, benches that are generously sprinkled with relaxed patrons enjoying the glorious view west across the wide sweep of the Hudson River to the cliffs of the Jersey side. About 2 miles to the north, or to the right for one sitting on a bench, is the unique superstructure of the George Washington Bridge, spanning the majestic river like a recently completed project from an erector set. The leisurely flow of traffic on the river completes this easel of Norman Rockwell-like beauty.

It is the first week of May, one of those glorious portents of the oncoming summer, perhaps the first day of the year suited for shirtsleeves. Sitting on one of the benches is an unassuming man of about 45 years of age. There is nothing that would call one's attention to this man, who seems to be little more than one of many people enjoying the elements and taking in the beautiful view cross the river to the Jersey horizon. He is looking, but he is not seeing. He is wrapped in his own thoughts due to a recent problem that has befallen him. Eventually, he closes his eyes, 10 seconds, 20, maybe more, so wrapped in his own thoughts is he.

Upon opening his eyes, he finds a handsome young man sitting a few feet away at the other edge of the bench. His leisurewear boasts the prestigious labels of our day and his forehead is crowned with the latest in elegant sunglasses at rest from its ocular duties. He is clean-shaven, well groomed, tanned and healthy under an impressive shock of chestnut hair.

A minute goes by, maybe 2. "Nice day, eh?" says the young man.

"Beautiful," says the bench's original inhabitant.

"Makes it great to be alive, doesn't it?"

"Yeah, I guess."

This initial salvo leads to more polite conversation, until the 2 men of our story have each other's confidence. They are getting along, passing the time pleasantly. Finally, the young man asks, "What's your name?"

"Alfred. And yours?"

"Jesus."

Alfred smiles. "I have a brother named Jesus. My grandfather came from Puerto Rico. His name was Alfredo and I was named for him, but Jesus is a common name amongst Latinos. Are you Latino?"

The young man lightly shakes his head and leans closer to Alfred, looking at him more intensely. "No, you don't get it. I **am** Jesus."

Alfred squints slightly, perplexed by such a declaration. "Yeah, and I'm Derek Jeter."

An awkward silence now intervenes on what had been an enjoyable bit of human interaction. Alfred's confidence in the other has been challenged. What is this guy up to?

"Jesus" notices an ugly scar on the forearm of Alfred closest to him. It is at least 6 inches long and disfigures the arm in a nasty way. "How'd you get that scar?"

Alfred is not sure whether to respond. Is this guy a kook – or what? Eventually, he answers. "An industrial accident."

"Jesus" moves a bit closer. "Give me your hand." Alfred recoils slightly, not sure what to do. "C'mon, don't be afraid." "Jesus" takes his hand and stretches the scarred arm out straight. "Leave your arm out." He then begins to run his index finger slowly across the scar. As the finger passes, the scar disappears, until it is completely gone. Alfred's jaw drops open like a hippo mouth, his eyes open wide. He takes back his arm and begins to examine the area where the scar used to be, running his own finger across it. His sense of touch finds nothing but healthy skin, including a manly amount of black hair. He looks up and stares at Jesus, trying to speak but unable to do so. His mouth moves like a fish out of water.

The young man is smiling as he says, "Jesus Christ, of Nazareth, glad to meet you Alfred." Alfred is dumbfounded, unable to react. His mouth continues to flap, still groping for speech. He looks away from Jesus, towards the silver structure of the George Washington Bridge. A slow barge is passing under it, but Alfred sees neither the bridge nor the barge.

Jesus has moved back to his edge of the bench. He is looking towards the west, staring at an apartment complex crowning the Jersey Palisades on the other side of the river. "You know Alfred; I sat down here because you seemed to be troubled. What's the problem?"

Alfred slowly returns his gaze to Jesus. He scrutinizes the handsome face for a moment and is about to speak when he has an epiphany. His face lights up with joy.

"Wow, I just thought of something!"

"Tell me."

"Well, you were right. Yesterday I found out I have an advanced case of pancreatic cancer. I've been feeling these sharp pains for about a year, but more frequently lately, so I finally went to the doctor. It's bad. I had no insurance, kept putting it off, and now it is too late. They give me no more than 6 months."

Jesus seems disappointed. "Oh – I see."

"But now," continues Alfred, exalted, "well, here you are. You're Jesus! You can do it!"

Jesus continues to stare out across the Hudson. "Tell me Alfred, how did you pay for the industrial accident?"

"Oh Christ – sorry – I'm still trying to pay that off."

Jesus crosses his legs and stretches his right arm along the backrest of the bench. He lowers his expensive sunglasses – Oakleys – onto his eyes. He is elegant and relaxed, like a movie star at a Malibu beach house. "Alfred, I'm going to ask you a question. How many people do you know, in the whole world, who can do what I just did? I mean, we're talking **miracles** here."

"Uhh –," he is still unsettled by all this, "well, I'd say – nobody."

"Very good. I'm sure you know, Alfred, that they are paying some dudes millions of dollars to field ground balls up in the Bronx, and you expect me to perform miracles for nothing?"

Alfred is confused, bewildered. A slight headache begins to insinuate itself. He rubs his eyes, trying to find some sense in all this. "But you just erased my scar."

Jesus smiles. "That was an introductory offer."

"But Jesus, I'm barely making it, child support, rent – "

"You should have thought of that when you dropped out of high school."

"What?" Alfred is beginning to get angry. "Who the fuck are you? What are you up to?" He begins to get up, menacingly, a scowl on his face.

Jesus is still relaxed, in control. "Now get it together. Sit down and behave. I am Jesus Christ, you cannot harm me." Alfred continues to stare at Jesus. He eventually sits down and calms himself, realizing this is his last chance and does not want to blow it. Jesus continues, "Look Alfred, you see that guy jogging towards us over there?" Alfred looks to his right and sees a man of about 60, thinning grey hair, slightly overweight, with sweat pants and a purple NYU tee shirt.

"Yeah, in fact, he looks familiar. I think I worked painting his apartment about a year ago. What a place he has, view of the river, a palace."

"Right. He made a fortune in coffee futures."

"Coffee futures? You mean he grows coffee, or sells coffee, or has plantations?"

"No. Really, he has nothing to do with coffee. He pushes paper, messes with computers, I don't think he has to leave his apartment anymore."

"And you can make millions like that?"

"Tens of millions. Anyhow, about 5 years ago he had big problems with his prostate. He paid me plenty to get it done."

Alfred sighs deeply, sits back on the bench and begins shaking his head slowly. In an almost subconscious way, he begins to realize Jesus is not on his side, that he will not help him. But he still clings to a sliver of hope. "But Jesus – you're Jesus! You're supposed to – "

Jesus cuts him off brusquely. "Alfred, do you know why Christians are now the most potent force in the world, why they have the best technology, the most wealth, the most goods and services, the strongest military power and the dominant role in the world?" Alfred is now defeated. He shrugs. "I'll tell you why Alfred. Because Christians compete! Because Christians have ambition, they push themselves, force each other, and make it get better. They are constantly struggling with each other and everyone else and driving the culture forward. That's why!"

Alfred says nothing. He stares blankly towards the Jersey side, not even noticing the long, slow barge that recently passed under the George Washington Bridge going by his position on the upper west side of Manhattan. He then has one last thought, one last card to play. He turns to Jesus.

"But Jesus, I understand all that. I understand I'm not the smartest guy around, that I've made my mistakes, that I could have done things different. I understand. I don't deserve a big house or fancy apartment. I can't take vacations at luxury resorts or eat in gourmet restaurants. No Lexus, no designer clothes. I get it. But Jesus, I'm sick! Surely you can't believe I have to compete for a cure the same way you pay for a luxury box at Yankee Stadium. Jesus – I work, I'm not a deadbeat, never have been. C'mon Jesus" – his voice trails off, not knowing what more to say.

Jesus uncrosses his legs and sits up straight, removing his forearm from the backrest. He stretches, settles back and begins straightening his clothes. With a sigh, he looks out at the passing barge. He seems bored.

Alfred turns away, leans forward and puts his head in his hands, rubbing his forehead with the tips of his fingers. He stops rubbing after about 10 seconds but continues to slump forward, looking down at the ground. "You know Jesus, you're not anything like I thought you'd be. In fact, you seem more like the devil to me." When there is no response, Alfred looks up. The bench beside him is empty.

The sun is beginning to set behind the Jersey heights. The sky is lavishly smudged with deep shades of red and orange, which reflect stunningly off the Hudson River. Further up in the sky, the first stars are beginning to appear. It is very beautiful.

Eight months later, Alfred died.

This is the Jesus Rush Limbaugh's attitude conjures up. I'd call that the Anti-Christ and millions of fervent Christians are worshipping it.

Relevant Material: *"Everything is in the soul of a worker. They have moved the world. (–) The musical poetry of Beethoven, the delicate sonnets of Shakespeare – it has all been created with the skin of the people, because without these columns of effort, without that substratum of blood, nothing would be in place." From the quasi-novel "Mortal y Rosa" (Young and Mortal) by the Spanish genius, Francisco Umbral.*

PART V

THE ARTS, SPORTS, POP CULTURE, HOW WE AMUSE OURSELVES

OLYMPIC CLICHES

Being that the Olympics have arguably become the single-most important event on the human calendar, rather than feel guilt for writing yet another essay on the subject, I shall consider such expanded treatment unavoidable for one such as I, possessed of a mind in perpetual mental ebullience. Having already discussed the unobjective nationalistic aspects of media coverage, allow me to roam into other areas of media critique. Let's face it, when the day is done and the kids are finally put to bed, the Olympics are whatever the media makes them out to be.

As we all know, NBC was responsible for the dissemination of Atlanta '96. No one can undertake an enterprise of this magnitude and please everyone. This writer can only commend the network for its announcers, commentators, athletic experts and technical work. (I especially liked Cris Collingsworth's work in Track and Field.) Other than the usual bitch as to excessive patriotic bluster, my primary complaint centers on NBC's concept of the Games and how they presented them.

This essay was inspired by a commentary made on National Public Radio. I feel somewhat guilty for not remembering the name of the journalist responsible for my inspiration, but his cogent remarks had to do with NBC's decision to give us more "soap opera" than sport. Bingo! What we got was theater, melodrama, innumerable contrived bits of heroism and dedication to the detriment of actual sports coverage. The manufactured human-interest angle took precedence over the sporting activities themselves. Rather than athletic competition, we got "The Lou Gehrig Story," "Brian's Song," "Fear Strikes Out" or "Hoosiers." It was as if we were watching a dramatic documentary of the Atlanta Games rather than the Games themselves. What we were really seeing was "schmaltz."

As a result of this attitude, some unusual sports we might never see anywhere else, like badminton, judo, Ping-Pong and others, were given virtually no coverage. Most prejudiced by this "schmaltz" concept were the team competitions, which produced some of the most dramatic moments of these Games. A few examples are the Cuba-USA baseball game, where the underdog American college kids almost rallied to beat the supposedly invincible Cuban machine; the outstanding men's soccer final, where Nigeria surprised soccer power Argentina in a memorable battle; the bitterly contested softball final won by the American women over their now arch rivals, China. All of these events were given the "highlight" treatment instead of the actual game, or, at the very least, some live coverage. But of all the errors made by NBC, the most glaring was their quasi-coverage of the splendid woman's soccer final.

The Gold Medal game in woman's soccer filled the University of Georgia's football stadium with 78,000 rabid fans. It was one of the most eagerly awaited events Atlanta '96 had to offer, being a rematch of a scoreless tie in the preliminary round. It turned out to be a tense battle that lived up to its billing, the Americans finally winning by a score of 2 to 1.

Unfortunately, NBC, in keeping with its soap opera format, gave us a few minutes of match highlights and fifteen minutes profiling America's top player. Instead of the exciting environment of this outstanding game, we got something like this:

" ... overcome the most unbeatable odds to become the athlete she is today. Trish Kelly Shannon lost her mother on the day she was born, leaving her fate in the hands of her troubled father, an unemployed whaler, who unwittingly introduced her to the game of soccer at the tender age of two when he drop kicked her out a second story window and then disappeared. Miraculously having survived the fall, Trish was sent to live with an indifferent aunt who had a hairy wart on the tip of her nose. Abused and neglected, beset with acute halitosis and heartbreaking outbreaks of psoriasis, the lonely young girl began angrily kicking anything in sight in what the psychiatrists later defined as "subliminal revenge syndrome," more commonly known as "being fucked up." As the roulette wheel of life would have it, a phys-ed teacher at her junior high, a Mr. Wartmuller, noticing Trish's rabid obsession for kicking things, as well as the debut of her adolescent chest, turned her on to soccer – and generally turned her on – before eventually going to jail for the crime of Statutory Foreplay. The susceptible young girl, still struggling to conquer a severe infatuation with oral sex, would go on to become the greatest player the sport has ever known. Now having achieved her life long dream, that being a shoe deal with a well known company, she has dedicated herself to finding her dad, who she would like to kick where it hurts the most, and then thank for all he did for her ..."

Or how about the heartwarming story of the fifty pound American gymnast, Shannon Trish Kelly, who came back to win a medal in Atlanta after having tragically missed her event in Barcelona when nobody told her she was a girl ...

Or the incredible dedication of swimmer Kelly Shannon Trish, who has logged so much time in the pool she can't remember what it's like to feel wet ...

Being that NBC decided on vaudeville over sport, these Olympics broke the record for clichés, soon to be broken at the Republican national convention in San Diego. As a result of Atlanta '96, we now know that just about every athlete competing in the Olympics was "on a mission," or had "worked all my life for this moment," or had "a dream come true." It is now transparently obvious (how could we have been so ignorant?) that nobody should "ever give up," that if you "just keep trying, you can be whatever you want to be," and that you must "believe in yourself."

My personal favorite had to do with "sacrifice." We were constantly being told how this or that athlete had "sacrificed so much for this moment." I remember an ESPN announcer wrapping up after the American women had won the gold in basketball. He talked about how much they had "sacrificed" over the last year to reach their goal. I heard a similar statement from the star pitcher on America's triumphant softball team. I eventually had to stop and ask ... sacrifice?

Imagine being a young man or woman in your early 20's with an outstanding skill in baseball, basketball or soccer. Undoubtedly you want nothing more than to play your sport at the highest level against and with people just like yourself. Continue to imagine that someone comes up to you and says ... hey! ... you're on the team and for the next two years you can play ball everyday at somebody else's expense, everything taken care of, just get ready for the Olympics ... the best food, lodging, coaching, facilities ... just get ready. And then imagine, on top of all that, the opportunity to travel all over the world, playing your sport, everything taken care of, Europe, Asia ... just play ... imagine that.

"Gee thanks, but I have a job back at the car wash, maybe you should find someone else. I don't think I can make the 'sacrifice' ..."

As I put a wrap on my Atlanta '96 experience, like a flooded river that eventually finds its original course, I always come back to a similar conclusion: In much the same way modern Christianity now reflects rather than effects secular western culture (see essay "Michael Chang or Christians Revisited"), so it is with the modern Olympic Games. Its supposed creed of goodwill, harmony and rosy-cheeked dimples, has all but been smothered under an avalanche of competitive ferocity hell bent on personal glory. Being a nice person seems to have been lost in this quest for individual greatness. Nothing could more reflect the current ethic of the predominant western mind set.

Being nice is more important than being great. How about putting that in the Olympic creed.

WHO KILLED LADY DI?

I begin writing this essay just a few days after the tragic death of one of the greatest myths ever nurtured by Occidental society. Having already written negatively about the Lady Di-like persona (see essay "Lady Di"), her needless, horrifying demise caused me to reflect even more – and not without a vaguely felt indigestion of guilt – on who she was and what she meant.

Judging from the vaudeville of unreliable sources available to an average citizen, I did not dislike Diana Spencer and would never have wished the sad fate that awaited her. As one who does not even believe in the execution of violent criminals, I mourn the passing of this woman in the same way I'd mourn the death of any human being so senselessly deprived of their right to live, of children deprived their mother, of parents deprived their daughter, of friends deprived of friends. But this is as far as my sympathy goes. I do not approve the role she was given to play in the burlesque of western culture, and consider her death a direct karmic result of that role. The fact that she died while fully immersed in the ramifications of her life style has a mathematical perfection hard to deny, in much the same way a gangster might die in a shoot out.

Before resolving the crime in question, there are other pressing considerations to ponder.

In analyzing the circumstances that led to this tragedy, much has been made of the role of the press and the right to privacy of people like Diana Spencer. Not having entered any popularity contests, I find no difficulty in saying that I don't have much respect for the privacy of people playing such roles in the world. One cannot expect to live such a lavish life style while having done so pitifully little to earn it, without there being a price to pay. The price paid by Diana Spencer, I agree, was much too high and can be chalked up to some awfully bad luck (and karma). But the loathsome pursuit of the crass "paparazzi" is a part of the aggravation quotient to be garnered from such a way of life. I reserve such feelings not only for the parasitical Lady Di-Jackie K's of the world, but for the pop star-cinema idol-athletic hero segment of our culture as well. Don't expect me to worry about the privacy of people living in such dubious extravagance.

There is the insinuation that much of what has just been said is mitigated by the great "humanitarian" work done by the deceased. It is now evident that in between leisure jaunts to Corsica or the south of France, or when she was not busy at the hair dresser or occupied with her favorite fashion designer or dining at the Ritz with Sheik Ali-Ali, the richest man this side of Kensington Palace, she could find time to cheer up the troops in Bosnia, lend herself to the fight against AIDS, or even have her picture taken with Mother Teresa. Not only that, she was against land mines, which is quite a coincidence, because I hate land mines too! ... and oh, yeah, I almost forgot; she really loved her children. I'll have to ask my mother if she loved us as much as Diana Spencer loved hers.

I'd like to remind the reader that such charitable work and humanitarian stances are an integral part of a princess's "job." The much-maligned Prince Charles, her publicly scorned, generally reviled ex-husband, is not lacking in such causes. If one is to objectively weigh the evidence here, the great "humanitarian" qualities of Diana Spencer might have something to do with the fact that she is somewhat more attractive than the average princess. One has to wonder if an ugly princess could ever be the humanitarian Lady Di was.

Now, who killed Lady Di?

There is an amorphous, mercury-like substance formlessly making its way through the environment that might be referred to as the "general public." This implacable, insatiable herd, through some instinctive homing device, made its way to London by the millions this weekend in order to say farewell to their fallen goddess.

This ambiguous stew is the defendant in this case.

The "herd" is a very complex entity whose underground springs of subconscious behavior can be very difficult to get a reading on. At this evolutionary juncture in time, each individual head in the herd is so lacking the self esteem necessary to be a truly whole person, is so insecure with regard to their own personal worth, they must create mythical people to live vicariously through, someone who is their embodiment of perfection, the outlet for all their unfulfilled hopes and frustrations, someone they wish they could be. The vast majority of this herd are the same people who impatiently wait for the next bit of gossip and the latest round of forbidden photos. The despicable, omnipresent "paparazzi," so idiotically chasing after the Diana Spencers of the world, is employed by the "general public." The herd demands their product and pays their salary.

If what has just been said above can be accepted by the reader, it might be said that the "general public" is guilty of something like Involuntary Manslaughter. As the District Attorney in this case, I want more. In this jurisdiction, we believe the more severe crime of Murder, with its accusation of intent to kill, is more appropriate.

We live in a society that prostrates itself before the false Gods of triumph, "success," being #1, and a whole host of egotistical pursuits. The Newtonian reaction to this attitude is the creation of substantial amounts of envy, jealousy, resentment, and other such negative residues left over for the losers in this societal scheme. For every "winner" there is a "loser," and a society based so heavily upon competitive forces cannot escape this kind of polarization.

The love shown by the herd for Diana Spencer is genuine, but it is not the only manifestation of human feeling involved. Deep down in the herd's collective subconscious, as they change dirty diapers and deal with screaming kids, as they blindly trudge off to the job early each day, as they get shit-faced in front of the weekend soccer match on the "telly," there are doses of envy, jealousy and resentment in play as well. The harassment of people like Diana Spencer is the revenge of the "general public." Like an idolized bullfighter who could only satisfy his adoring public by taking more and more risks, so it was with Diana Spencer, **Lady Di!** The more the herd needed to love her, to adore her, to follow her example, the more of her they wanted for themselves. They eventually took everything she had.

I say guilty of murder. Let the jury decide.

In the end, the whole idea of a "Lady Di" is a vulgar concept created by and for the vulgarity that reigns over western culture. In spite of all her efforts, Lady Di was eventually done in by this chronic vulgarity.

Relevant Material: *"Charity! What good did it do? It kept poor people miserable as they awaited a few crumbs to momentarily soothe their hunger in order to prolong their bondage."*

"Charity was selfishness disguised as virtue; the sacrifice of a very small part of the superfluous, distributed at somebody's whim. Charity, no: Justice!"

"Charity had never done anything to dignify mankind."

"It was the most impotent and anemic of all the virtues." From the novel "La Bodega" (The Wine Cellar), by the immortal Spaniard, Vicente Blasco Ibanez.

"If you know how to face failure and triumph, treating these two imposters the same way ..." From the poem "If," by the incomparable Rudyard Kipling.

THE KING AND WHO?

(This essay was written around 2000 in Spain)

When Ronald Reagan became President, it seemed to be the culmination of a process that had become, over the course of post-war history, inevitable. None of this fatality had to do with Reagan's political philosophy, but with who he was before entering politics and what it takes to be successful at it. The fact that an actor had become President was the closing of a circle that had arrived from different directions.

There was a perfection here that seemed truly geometric.

The television age drastically changed our concept of reality, including everything from the hyper-consumption of the global economy to the way we do politics ... and just about everything else. With the advent of TV, politics has become another form of stay at home entertainment, not much different from the Simpsons, MTV, Shaquille O'Neal, or The News itself. What you can do in front of a camera has probably become a greater element of success for a politician than whatever the candidate thinks about Alan Greenspan, the Middle East or "affirmative action." Nowadays, in order to be President, you must also be a large part actor.

I had a similar revelation this year in Spain, when it suddenly became apparent that 2 wildly divergent roles had finally come together, closing a circle that had been stretching towards each other for quite some time now, just as actor and President had. The eventual convergence of the 2 people representing these roles is an even more symbolic postulation of the contemporary human condition, with broader implications than the actor-president fusion.

Before revealing the participants in this convergence, some background is necessary.

In Spain, as in almost all the rest of the world, the great sporting passion is "futbol" (soccer). The daily newspaper with the largest circulation is something called Marca, which is devoted exclusively to sports. Even in the dead of summer, when the world of "futbol" takes its brief holiday in the blinding glare of the indolent Mediterranean beach culture, ¾ of this thick publication is devoted to "futbol" – a bit of basketball, tennis, cycling, track and field, and other assorted side show condiments, but nothing comes close to arousing the passions of the masses like ...

"Futbol"!

The primary focus of all this passion is the league season, known as La Liga. Its championship is the most cherished prize. But there is another competition that runs concurrently with this called "La Copa del Rey" (The King's Cup), which is a big deal as well.

All the major soccer leagues of Europe have tournaments like "La Copa del Rey." The most famous of all these events is the F.A. Cup (Federation Association Cup) in England. These tournaments have one quality above all else: they give the little guy a chance to measure himself against the Gods of their sport.

The competition for "La Copa" begins at a low level of organized Spanish football and eventually works its way up to the "Big Leagues" of the First Division, where such mythical clubs as Real Madrid and the Barcelona Football Club militate. If such a tournament were to exist in American baseball, it would start at the lowest rungs of the professional Minor Leagues, eventually reaching such heights of common man fantasy as the Yankees or Dodgers. Obviously, as the yearly event wears on, the little guys start to fall like ducks in hunting season. But on those rare, legendary occasions, the plebian torch bearers of us regular folks – whose real jobs are not "futbol," whose wives don't look like movie stars, who play on dirt fields in five thousand seat stadiums named for the one guy who's ever had enough interest to be the local sporting club's President – every once in awhile, something might happen that seems to carry the hand of God. Maybe you only managed one shot at some superior team's goal and ... miracle! ... the ball ricochets off a defender's hip, the goal tender slips on a rain soaked field, and for the next 80 minutes you defend your goal like a mother bear with cubs, and the referee blows the whistle, and you get a chance to play a First Division team, and ...

... 30 years later you're telling your grandson how you only lost 0-3 to Racing de Santender; "that's right Juanito, I played against Racing de Santender."

Perhaps the only thing comparable to it in American sport is the Boston Marathon, where the guy you see jogging in the park gets to run with Olympic champions.

The last game of the Spanish football season is always the final of "La Copa." By then, all the truck drivers who still play some football have been rudely dispatched and only the "big boys" are left. The stadium will be filled with tens of thousands of lunatic fans all dressed in their team colors. The King himself, in a rare appearance at such a proletarian venue, will watch the festivities from the Royal Box. At the conclusion of the game, he will present his own trophy (La Copa) to the winning squad, who will gallantly climb an Everest of stadium stairs in order to receive the royal gift from His Majesty's own hands.

The King is one of the participants mentioned above.

If the modern concept of royalty does not consider a monarch a liaison with God, these people do, theoretically, still represent the optimal virtues of their nation's idea of citizenry (for more, see essay "Lady Di" and "La Boda"). For a King such as Juan Carlos of Spain, this would entail a well rounded education, an appreciation of the arts, a virile physical training, a well groomed, noble bearing, impeccable honor and integrity, a devotion to the virtues of monogamous love and harmonious family life, etc. He is the embodiment of what every Spaniard should aspire to in their personal life and in their responsibilities to the community.

Sharing the Royal Box this year with his Royal Highness was a fellow who owns one of the teams in the final. I have decided not to mention his name (nor his team) because what will be said of him is, if not incriminating, very unflattering. Normally, my appetite for exposing such truth is comparable to a lion chomping into a fresh cut of wildebeest fricassee, but this fellow is not your average wildebeest. He is quite capable of sending someone with a swarthy complexion and hands the size of a pizza pallet to snuff out the life of anyone who crosses him. In fact, now that I think of it, none of this really happened this year ... no, it's just a Cup Final that happened ... oh God, who can remember.

The owner of this team is the other participant mentioned above.

This man is the prototype of what we call a "gangster." The Spanish government has been trying to put him in jail seemingly since the days of the Spanish Armada. He is the kind of guy who drips gold chains and belches in public. His head is a bulbous, balding protrusion smeared with a nose that seems to have been target practice a few times too many back in his youthful days in the "barrio." He is somewhat of a cross between Sancho Panza and Rodney Dangerfield and has all the class of a six-pack of Old Milwaukee beer (in cans). He now rules a dubious empire centered in the biggest and most glamorous resort city on the Costa del Sol (or one of those "Costas").

When I saw this man standing shoulder to shoulder with **The King** in his Royal Box ... well ... it seemed like the cosmic balance had now been broken. There were palm trees at the South Pole, the Amazon had frozen over; Pavarotti was singing rap, and Pamela Anderson was playing Lady Macbeth; the Hindus were eating at McDonald's and the sacred cows roamed the Pampas untouched.

But, upon further reflection, like an actor becoming President, it all began to make sense.

The reason why The King and the gangster have finally been so officially and publicly brought together is, not surprisingly, money. Money has had some positive impacts on the human condition. Before the widespread use of money, power and wealth were concentrated in control of the land. Very few people had access to this source of wealth. You couldn't spend it or carry it around with you. You couldn't trade a square meter of land for a goat. Money has allowed more people to get in on the fun. It has democratized things and now the boy from the "barrio" uses the same after-shave as The King.

But when The King and the gangster begin to socially interact in an atmosphere of normality, it perhaps signals something more fundamentally negative. It means the end of morality as represented by anything other than money. It means money has become everything. It might not be an overstatement to say that the procurement of money, especially vast sums of money, does not bring out our best qualities.

A world ruled exclusively on principles dictated by money, might very well be a world ruled by scoundrels.

JANET'S BOOB

(2/04)

I feel somewhat ambivalent about the now historical halftime incident at this year's Super Bowl, where a sacred part of Janet Jackson's anatomy was briefly exposed to the world. I'm not here to say that it was the proper forum for such an act, but the severe seismic jolt it has sent through our culture, considering the severity of the "crime," seems even more ridiculous.

There is always an era in any great imperial power's rise and fall where its dominance and hedonistic manifestations reach its apex. In the case of the United States, this era began at the conclusion of WW II and still seems to be ascending, although this latest Bush Oil War and the financial pressures it is putting on the enterprise known as the United States – without even mentioning the universal ill will it is engendering against the Empire – might be the summit in this climb. Whether the American nation can find a more benevolent and constructive way to use its power – which, ironically, would help to preserve rather than weaken its strength – still remains to be seen. But that's another story.

Perhaps no regular cultural event on the American calendar more represents this muscular, imperial braggadocio than the Super Bowl, along with the sport that gave birth to it, American football. As the vaudeville of its presentation has evolved, the elements of merciless physical violence as manifested by the Pavlovian conditioned monsters on the field, and the sexual innuendo embodied in the bouncing siliconed cleavage of the cheerleading nymphs on the sidelines, have joined hands in the Circus Maximus of the 21st century. All this violence and sexual energy, which is diffused over many games during the regular season, is focused in one great gladiatorial event on Super Bowl Sunday. This is the golden era of Rome, the Pax Romana of the Emperor Augustus in its most shrill, plebeian form.

Although the exposure of Janet's boob took everyone by surprise, the fact that it took place at this floozy-like display of contemporary American culture is, upon some reflection, far less surprising.

In trying to make sense of American society's reaction to all this, one finds it difficult to not see a tremendous amount of cynicism and hypocrisy. If we examine the Godzilla-like proportions of the sex business in America, this fact is put into better focus. Through some information source that has now faded from memory, it was recently brought to my attention that the porno industry now moves more money than all of pro sports combined. I'll give the reader some time to digest that fact ... before mentioning that some of the world's most powerful, respected corporate organizations are growing fat feeding at the all-you-can- eat buffet of these erotic enterprises. First and foremost here are the gigantic communications beasts – names like Viacom, Comcast, AT&T, etc. – whose cable TV and Internet operations provide this glut of manufactured breasts and panting sluts, complete with a limber array of acrobatic positions in a professional smorgasbord of the sexual act. Cunts, cocks, tits and ass in an ever growing avalanche of erotic debauchery whose satiation point still seems way beyond any discernible horizon.

Another extremely respected part of the global economy's infrastructure found gorging itself on sexual profiteering is the "hospitality" industry. This is a euphemism for those who shelter us from the elements both on vacation and business trips. The average American male seems to go into an alley cat rut once he is within the privacy and disconnect of his away from home hotel room. A good pull on the pole with the visual fantasies made real on a TV screen is a lot cheaper and less complicated than the hire of some live female flesh. As a result, such impeccable corporate citizens as Sheraton, Hilton, Marriott, Doubletree, Holiday Inn, Ritz-Carlton, etc., along with all their subsidiaries of cheaper hotels and weigh stations for the weary traveler, as well as any conglomerate giants that may include them in their holdings, are creaming in their pants (ha, ha) with money earned in collusion with the purveyors of porn. Although I cannot offer up this next comment as a hard-core fact, I seem to remember hearing that the mountain of money earned from the masturbatory client has now become an important, if not exclusive element in the profit margin of the lodging business.

Now, before someone starts complaining that there is a big difference between a free-willed adult amusing himself in a private place (are there such places left, or are the "security" cameras rolling here too?) and Janet's boob being shown before the largest TV audience of the year, I say "hold on a minute ..."

Yes, the distinction can be made. But when we juxtapose this thoroughly rain soaked terrain of sexual permeation against the few seconds of Janet's peek-a-boo titillation, we see that her actions were not performed in a vacuum. They rest upon a strong erotic foundation that has been constructed with the acquiescence of some of the most respected players in the global economy, and fed by the likes of John Q. American.

OK, let's get serious. What provided the spark for this essay occurred while watching ESPN SportsCenter two days after "the event." Although I did not see the act as it happened, in the less than 48 hours since it took place I had seen the quasi-impaired rendition of it on various TV outlets at least 20 times. Just 10 minutes into the SportsCenter in question, it had already been shown 3 or 4 more times, with the usual outrage and consternation – Paul Tagliabue explaining, Janet Jackson apologizing, CBS explaining, Justin Timberlake contrite, MTV explaining – alright already! The KKK was beginning to look like a wholesome, family values organization compared to anyone connected with this Super Bowl.

When they finally decided to move on to something else (they got back to Janet later), it was a rundown of the best hockey fights from this or that ... who knows, but they showed extensive footage of this Neanderthal activity. Hockey fights can be some of the more gruesome spectacles on ice, air, land or sea. Fighting on skates is a very precarious endeavor; a slip here, a loss of balance there, a sweater pulled over one's eyes and voila! ... one of the moronic participants finds himself in a very compromised position. This means his foe gets to pummel him gleefully with a deluge of unanswered blows until whoever is responsible for this business enterprise deems it appropriate to stop the slaughter. (This usually happens about the time the loser's face begins to resemble a ½ pound of chopped meat.) I phrase it in such a way because the hockey business actually sells itself with such exhibitions, which are no more than organized dog fights with human contestants.

Unlike the Janet Jackson story, which was painted over a background of self-righteous indignation and outrage, the hockey fights were given to us with all the light-hearted banter of a Leno monologue. This was family fun. Nobody was hastily rushing the kids out of the room or hiding such "filth" behind the techno defenses of the "parental discretion" button. Boys will be boys. "Junior" might even find a role model here.

Perhaps <u>I'm</u> the "pervert," the sick person, the one who needs spiritual guidance and rehabilitation, but I'm going to make the following confession anyway: I found this medley of hockey fights far more offensive than Janet's 2 seconds of shame. If a son or daughter of mine had to eventually stumble upon something I'd rather they not be exposed to, I'd much prefer it to be Janet's boob than these semi-programmed dog fights the hockey business deems necessary for its survival.

If we strip all the meat from the bone and get to the nub of it all, we find that human beings only truly respond to 3 things, and in this order: hunger, sex, violence. Unlike the first two, which are biological needs that must be appeased, violence is environmentally influenced and caused in greater part by hunger and, to a lesser degree, by sexual tension. In the modern world of plenty, the violence caused by hunger has been displaced somewhat by the violence caused by poor living conditions. Violence is not necessary. Violence is spurred on by frustration. Human beings cannot only live without violence, they would really prefer to. Most people will try to avoid it at all costs.

Once we get to the point where that hockey fight is considered more obscene than Janet's boob, we might really be able to say that our species has moved on to a better place.

THE MOST OVERRATED MOVIE EVER MADE

(5/06)

Unlike the vast majority of the herd living on the other side of my front door who make cinema a regular element in their lives, my zeal for the motion picture has dried to the point where it can barely be called a trickle. I've been chastised for this abstention by people whose minds function in a way I can only admire and respect; intellectually impressive people who assure me of the existence of worthwhile films in abundance, you have to know where to look, etc. and hidy ho. I have the utmost faith in their opinions, but my evolution away from the cinema habit goes beyond the generally vapid nature of those films most present for mass consumption, and into the realm of simple physical distaste for the experience. Do I have to apologize for not liking to sit in one place for almost 3 hours in a huge, hermetically sealed, inky dark room, whose front wall is filled with a nuclear blast of light and color, all accompanied by a sound track whose volume could knock over a sumo wrestler?

If so, I apologize.

As explained in previous essays, this was not always so. At one time I was an ardent "cinephile," there hardly being a week lacking my attendance at movie theaters scattered throughout the landscape of my existence. Even now, in spite of my general lack of interest, the motion picture is such an integral part of modern life, the ability to completely ignore it is almost impossible – even for me.

You don't like football? Try ignoring the Super Bowl.

It might not be an exaggeration to say that one of the most renowned movies in the history of the art form carries the name *Forrest Gump*. It has been universally accepted as a movie classic, a masterpiece, a legendary icon of cinema brilliance. It hogged almost all the industry buzz the year of its release, won all the awards, this Globe, that Oscar, "I'd like to thank ...," yeah, yeah. If it were a baseball player, it would be a definite Hall of Famer.

Having never seen this film, when the opportunity recently presented itself on TV, I plopped myself down in front of it.

The erosion of my sympathy for *Forrest Gump* was far from immediate. It is a skillfully done film that entices the viewer with a combination of beauty, excellent story telling and stellar performances by a talented cast. But as the epic tale grinded through its torturous course, it slowly became evident to me that its supposedly neutral, objective look at an era, was an elaborately disguised vehicle for a very conservative (maybe even reactionary) message.

Before getting on to that, there are some more nibbling appetizers to start with.

When it comes to works of artistic creation, a strict adherence to reality is not an essential element of consummation. Depending on how a work is presented, varying degrees of "poetic license" can not only be the proper course to take, but what makes it successful. Being that we are talking about cinema here, I'll give 2 such examples from 2 of my favorite films: neither the somewhat demented, mega-hawkish General played by George C. Scott in *Dr. Strangelove*, nor the emotionally collapsed, paranoid, neurotic police detective played by Alan Arkin in *Little Murders*, are realistically believable characters. But they are perfect for the satirical black humor of the movies they appear in.

The movie *Forrest Gump* does not present itself in such a fashion. It is meant to be a fairly faithful representation of a real era in history, an era we are all familiar with. The things that happen are supposedly tied to a reality we should believe. I begin to lose respect for such a film when it's most important character becomes an All American football star without ever having played a down of football in his life. Likewise, his later ascension to the top of the table tennis world is even more absurd. How am I supposed to take this film seriously?

But the main course of my critical disdain for *Forrest Gump* is its intellectual message. My guess is that most *Forrest Gump* fans never even thought it had a socio-political message. In fact, it seemed to be painfully trying to not take sides. But a more sensitive investigation of its content reveals something quite different.

My first pangs of uneasiness began to stir during the Vietnam War footage. Obviously, *Forrest Gump* did not try to justify the war or portray it as something positive, but it maintained a kind of neutrality that differed from the generally negative attitude of the few serious films dealing with this unfortunate interlude in American history. It treated the war as if it were just something that happened.

OK. I can accept that. This horse has been beaten enough.

But then it proceeded to show its true colors. In trying to bob and weave its way through the minefields of blame, the film *Forrest Gump* has nary a judgmental attitude towards anything. The only exception to this is how it portrayed the anti-war, counter culture of longhaired, unkempt young people – hippies and such – who played a fundamental role in blowing the whistle on the fiasco in S.E. Asia.

In watching this film, I had a dim feeling that the author may have tried to temper his distaste for this counter-culture that challenged the idyllic image of America's purity, but his true feelings could not be contained. The anti-war demonstrators wore the black hat in this movie. They were portrayed as reckless, insincere, as spoiled brats and hypocrites, as something ominous and dangerous.

The primary vehicle used to promote this unsavory view was the woman who became Forrest Gump's only love interest throughout his life, beginning in childhood. Being that Gump was never emotionally mature enough to consummate a true romantic relationship (though it didn't stop him from being a soldier), she is eventually forced to find her love life away from him. This leads her into the clutches of hippy culture; a reckless, irresponsible fling with drugs, sex and self-flagellation. The only person with a truly villainous role in this film is her boy friend, dressed ominously in black like a hippy version of an outlaw from a spaghetti western. As the years go by, her life begins to fall apart in an uncontrollable free fall of deprivation, until she almost jumps off a building in despair.

I think we can safely assume the author feels she made the wrong life choice.

Meanwhile, her mentally retarded friend has doodled along with nary a sophisticated thought in his sub-standard brain and blundered into being a millionaire shrimper. He's been a good boy. He's being rewarded for it.

Forrest Gump turns out to be a film that apologizes for the unsavory aspects of America's imperial personality, demonizes those who dare to question it, and makes a hero of a mentally sub-normal person who questions nothing and does exactly as he's told. This movie, in contrast to the agitation of the 60's and 70's and the uncertainty of the 80's, is telling America that everything is OK, that what we do and believe is good and righteous. Just carry on and be good boys and girls.

When a motion picture is so positively regaled and universally distributed as *Forrest Gump*, it can have some form of socio-political influence. Where have we gone since its release?

We've elected a president (George W.) who could easily be described as the Forrest Gump version of presidents. His government has had the arrogance to involve the nation in yet another third world war that is bleeding the country dry in a hapless effort that cannot succeed. Who will make the next "great film" that apologizes for this?

Perhaps it is not just a coincidence that *Forrest Gump* is a southern film. The tip in the balance of power that delivered the United States to the neo-cons occurred here. It was accomplished by pandering to the most provincial elements of this "Bible Belt," what I'd call *Forrest Gump* people.

A POST TIGER WORLD

(12/09)

Back in February of 2006 I wrote an essay called "A Business Opportunity" where I waxed poetically about that bigger than life icon of the American Dream, Tiger Woods. I will now re-create that passage in this essay, but before doing so I'll pat myself on the back for a sentence that was so prophetic – and the reader will surely recognize it – it's almost metaphysical. Did I jinx the fallen demy-god?

"One of the more magnetic personalities in the world these days is the undeniably best golfer in the world, Tiger Woods (for more, see essay "Tiger Robinson"). It is not often that an athlete of such extraordinary talent is coupled with a positive kind of charisma that translates into a bullet proof marketing infallibility. Talent, sex appeal, style, a droolable Swedish wife – Tiger is the whole package and more. With the help of his own good instincts and intelligence, he has been sold and packaged with a shrewdness bordering on perfection. Not being one to believe in anyone's image, I would take a certain degree of comfort if he were found one night in a cheap motel with a bag of blow and a crack whore.

That would truly be the end of the empire.

In any event, late one Sunday afternoon, I was potatoed up on the couch doing the zapper thing, when I caught a glimpse of Tiger strolling down a fairway. The beautiful off red color of his perfectly fitting shirt seemed Byronesque against the manicured emerald background of the golf course. I put the zapper down and decided to stay for awhile. I am not a golfer. This is a perfect example of Tiger Power at work."

Woo! It is not often one can find assertions of such discredited qualities. It ranks right up there with the Earth being the center of the universe or bloodletting as a cure. Tiger Woods, perhaps the most pristine representation of who we'd like to be, of what we envy; Tiger Woods, the maximum expression of a positive cultural product, has been found at the Bates Motel with his crack whore. At least I can say I had some inkling of this, that they didn't completely draw the shades on my good instincts. Maybe 95% –

We have now entered a Post Tiger World and, contrary to that stated above, it is not the end of the empire. In fact, it could be seen as an excellent educational opportunity for a culture that wallows neck deep in the lies and quasi-lies of marketing, advertising, public relations, image, politics, and the insincere hustle of neo-liberal capitalism in general. The fall of Tiger has hit our culture like an emotional act of terrorism. Who can we trust? Who's next? Mother Teresa?

It is good this has happened. It thaws the ice shelf of naiveté the American public has been frozen in for too long. With time, this ice shelf will probably freeze into numbness once again, but at least for now, maybe we've learned something.

The galactic distance between Woods' public persona and his private reality might not be unique in the human experience, but when such spectacular contradictions are embodied in a public figure of his stature, the shock value is historic. There is no need to go on about who or what this man represented in the global pop culture. The seismic jolt of the story speaks quite cheaply for that. I'll only add that a huge lie of this nature concentrated in a cultural hero of such Galahad proportions, could be unprecedented.

Woods, of course, is not the only mega-star to be given an image that most facilitates financial profit. But no one has ever been marketed as an emblem of human perfection more than him. Some of his apologists claim we, his public, are to blame, that we've created this myth from our own vicarious needs. This is a grossly overstated concept. To deny the massive investment in Tiger-creation by those profiting for and from him, is like denying he can hit a golf ball. Sure, we fell for it, and that is why we feel so violated. In a sense, we've been made fools of.

And really, isn't it the low quality of his transgressions that continue to fuel this inferno? Tiger Woods, the quintessence of style, class, self-confidence, intelligence, *savoir-faire* – Tiger Woods! – an almost laboratory creation of Horatio Alger triumph in the theater of American bullcrap, a validation of all we stand for, truth, liberty, justice, hi-yo Silver, away!

All of us, in our own mediocre, day in and day out way, understand the erotic pressures of life and how this can bring tension into our personal lives. We all understand how magnified such temptation can be for a person like

Tiger Woods, who's erotic possibilities could almost be described as infinite. If he had simply been too weak to defend himself from such temptation and had grudgingly succumbed to this tsunami of sexual availability few of us could ever imagine nor withstand, forgiveness would be a more plausible possibility.

What makes this so problematic for Woods is that his actions do not show him to be a weak person, but a BAD person, a cynical person, a completely self centered person unconcerned with those he might be hurting. Unlike other young men of his ilk – famous, rich, talented, attractive – who might give in to an incessant feminine assault that overwhelms their defenses, Woods seemed to be seeking these liaisons. He seemed to be as much of a catalytic agent as the women he was sleeping with (or how about "fucking"?). All this as a newlywed. All this when his beautiful wife was pregnant with his children. There is an element of self-indulgence here that is extremely unflattering, perhaps even repulsive. But self-indulgence in the absence of wickedness can be tolerated. This is hardly the case with Tiger Woods.

I'm lucky enough to have had some amorous experience with women who have fulfilled me in every way. Unfortunately (or fortunately, who knows?), none of these interludes lasted more than 5 years and, in truth, by the end of the second year or thereabouts, something began to be lacking. But we tried. In spite of these failures, the initial sincerity and the happiness it created were worth the experience. There are many variations on this theme and I do not consider my own history as far from average.

In the case of Tiger Woods, one has to wonder, in light of the evidence now piling up, if he was ever really sincere with this prototypical Swedish beauty he married, or was she just another calculated prop in the staging of the Woods image? Could marriage fidelity have ever been a serious consideration for this man? It seems to have been for his wife, which shines a very sour light of insincerity and cavalier disregard for others upon the great golfer.

And yet, this might not be the worst aspect of the Woods legacy. The villainous DNA of male infidelity can hardly be deemed a surprise as we stand upon the massive dung heap of human history proceeding this moment in the now. Even worse than being considered a cad, a rogue, a superficial playboy with little regard for others, is to be considered **stupid!**

Perhaps the most precious club in the Woods bag was his "intelligence." Smart. This guy is smart. He knows what he is doing. Stanford. He's got it all under control. Smart. If anyone might have pulled off such a double life, it could only have been Tiger. That's how smart he is.

That's how smart he was. Who's he smarter than now? Who's not smarter than him?

Many pundits believe once he returns to golf and starts winning again, many of these festering wounds will scab up and heal. If he can do that (if!) it would resolve a lot. This seems not implausible, but some scar tissue and disfigurement could be permanent. Here's why:

I have an acquaintance whose privacy (he deserves it Tiger) I'll protect with the simple name of Joe. Joe is a successful practitioner of our culture who's been married about 18 years, is raising a family and bringing home enough bacon to provide a lifestyle with the comforts and advantages most people would swoon for. His marriage, in my humble view, is neither good nor bad, but more correctly labeled typical. He has compromised with it, accepting both its joys and frustrations. He's hung in there, done what he's supposed to do, and, in truth, it ain't perfect, but it ain't bad.

One of the great rewards of Joe's life is to play golf at a posh country club. He's earned it. He plays well, like a 14 the last I asked. As one might imagine, until recently, Joe idolized Tiger Woods, put him on a pedestal of respect and envy at the limits such feelings might exist in a mature adult.

Such feelings no longer exist for Joe, and his attitude strongly suggests he is not coming back. His most telling words, the ones that have stuck with me from a more extensive diatribe, went something like this: "it's not like he was cheating on a middle aged wife he'd grown weary with, I mean, he'd hardly been married at all – and with what a piece of ass. He's a pig"!

One can understand Joe's attitude, no? There are millions of Joes out there and they are at the center of the Woods business demographic. Unlike LeBron's demographic, they have lots of money.

I repeat, this is good. The modus operandi of our culture is constantly making fools of us by those profiting the most (see health care non-reform). Wake up America, Tiger Woods is everywhere.

Relevant Material:

"Idolization is a form of possession, and possession is only consumed in destruction."

The author, speaking of his fame, says the following: "It's a mediocre misunderstanding. I am not who they think I am. They are not who they think they are. They dream they admire me. I dream they admire me. It's just a conjunction of dreams. Nothing exists."

These two remarks are from the quasi-novel Mortal y Rosa (I would translate this as "Young and Mortal"), by the Spanish genius Francisco Umbral.

THE WORLD'S BIGGEST ASSHOLE

(12/11)

If there is one thing contemporary human beings feel comfortable with it is lists, rankings, standings, some numerical representation of value that leaves no room for doubt. This is especially true in a complex world whose true functional mechanisms are shrouded in ambiguous subterfuges almost no one (no one?) can decipher (For more, see essay "Why People Like Sports"). The top ten, the best and worst dressed, our favorite foods, the five sexiest, the top ten hitters, the five best and worst plays, the most memorable moments, the best selling, the biggest failures, the Fortune 500, etc., etc. Who made the list? Who dropped off the list? Just give me a number, a poll, an inquest; just line it up in a way that is simple enough to understand – even for me.

People love lists.

When it comes to the world's top assholes, it is difficult to put a list together. The first inclination would be to accrue this difficulty to a fierce competition in the asshole community, one that would be hard to calibrate. Surprisingly, it is just the opposite. The world's top asshole has worn the crown for so long and by such a huge margin, that any list or poll has become irrelevant. He is an asshole's asshole, the quintessence of the word itself. He has no peers. He's cornered the market. He has a monopoly on it. His domination of the specialty would beat Usain Bolt in the 100-meter dash by 20 meters. What an asshole!

Donald Trump.

Being an asshole is something like being gay. Before my gay friends and readers get offended, this does not mean I think gay people are assholes. No. I'd guess the percentage and quality of "assholeness" in the gay community is no different than in the straight world. What I mean is that an asshole, with varying degrees of intensity and vocation, is born an asshole. (For the pro-life community, this means one becomes an asshole at conception). You cannot train to be an asshole. You cannot learn how to be an asshole. You cannot undo being an asshole. You cannot be cured of being an asshole. It comes naturally, like Willie Mays playing baseball. It is a life long affliction. Anything short of a lobotomy cannot change it. Only one thing can put an end to it – death.

If Donald Trump was an anonymous person and one was to investigate his life, I'm sure it would go something like this:

"So you knew him in the 6th grade"?

"Yeah – how could I forget Donnie? What an asshole. His big number was to fart out loud and fan the smell towards other people."

"So you knew Trump in the 11th grade"?

"Yeah – how could I forget an asshole like that? In the shower after gym class he'd give himself an erection and walk around making elephant noises."

"So you knew him in his early 20's"?

"Yeah – you don't forget assholes like that. He'd be sitting at the bar fawning over a lady and he'd point at another woman and say 'I fucked her'."

Boy, what an asshole.

All my grandparents came to the United States in the first decade of the 20th century. They eventually settled in Brooklyn where they started and raised their families. Anyone who grew up in Brooklyn with my parents' generation is familiar with the term "Trump Houses." It refers to thousands and thousands of housing units built by Donald Trump's father all across south Brooklyn, mostly in the form of small apartment buildings. Unlike his asshole son, who names everything he builds for himself, daddy Trump never called his housing projects Trump Houses. They just became such a fixture on the Brooklyn landscape; such a factor in the socio-economic development of an area, that the regular folks themselves began calling these buildings Trump Houses. It became a generic term that sprung up organically. It is a true testament to a man's life work.

Daddy Trump amassed a huge fortune building housing in Brooklyn. I'd guess it was a bigger fortune for its time than whatever The Asshole claims his worth is today. This is how Donald Trump got rich. He's been playing with house money all his life.

But hold on a minute. Rich kids can't be blamed for being rich and they have a right to be rich kids too. Being an asshole is no more or less prevalent amongst rich kids than other kids. Being an asshole cuts equally across all social barriers. Ted Turner, like Donald Trump, was born into an environment of financial well-being. His father made lots of money in advertising and publicity – mainly billboards and such – though when his son came of age his business was floundering. Yes, Ted Turner had a head start but he took advantage of it in a way that could be considered visionary. He was one of the first people to grasp the reality and potential of the new satellite technologies that led to cable TV. He just about invented 24-hour news. He's left an indelible mark on humanity. Assholes don't do that.

On the contrary, you could take away every shrill, tacky, adolescent, garish, ostentatious, tasteless, sophomoric project Donald Trump has ever built – the egotistical elephantine monuments to his undisputed reign as the World's Biggest Asshole – and the world would remain unchanged. In fact, doing away with whatever The Asshole has given us would improve the human condition.

I've often envisioned Donald Trump as the organizer and all around Big Kahuna of an annual Assholes Convention at one of his resorts or casinos or towers, whatever, at the most assholish project in his whole line of such projects. But, alas, this is not possible. It goes against the laws of the universe. There is no such thing as an asshole who knows he's an asshole. You cannot be an asshole unless you are unaware of it. You cannot aspire to be an asshole. No kid has ever told his mom and dad "when I grow up, I want to be an asshole." There is no empathy amongst assholes. There is no camaraderie amongst assholes. There is no solidarity amongst assholes. It is impossible for an asshole to walk up to another asshole and say,

"Hey man, it's an honor to meet an asshole like you; I've been wanting to meet you for a long time."

"Thanks, but the honor is all mine. Your reputation has preceded you and I can only envy an asshole of your credentials."

This cannot happen. You cannot herd assholes.

What a shame. Just think how much fun an annual Donald Trump Assholes Convention would be. But there is still hope – maybe he can organize a Donald Trump Hair Dressers Convention?

PART VI

OTHER STUFF

DISTINGUISHED PEOPLE

(5/07, Spain)

We often hear someone referred to as a "distinguished person." There is something in their presence, their bearing, the way they carry and present themselves, that defines them as such. Without even trying (if they had to, it would preclude them having it), they impose a kind of respect that others immediately feel and react to. They seem to carry an aura with them that is more felt than seen.

One of the nicest things anyone ever said about me is related to this concept. Before telling that story, some background is necessary.

The Spanish writer Juan Jose Millas has appeared in these pages before in the form of a translation of one of his newspaper articles (see essay, "Suicide, Guantanamo Style"). Millas, for those who haven't read the referred essay, is one of Spain's eminent satirists, his regular newspaper column being syndicated throughout the country. Like many of Spain's foremost journalists, he is also a first rate novelist. His latest is called "Laura and Julio," and it captured my utmost attention from the very first words. I cannot further expound upon this novel because, as I write, I've only read 20 pages of it. But there have already been a few passages that so resonated with me, they became the embryos for this essay. They now sit next to the notebook I am writing in, scratched onto a small piece of paper ripped from a notepad. I would normally underline the material, but the book was loaned to me by another person who has appeared in these pages, my literary guru in Spain, the Catalan gentleman, Pepin Mari. No distinguished person would ever consider scribbling into another's book.

The novel in question revolves around a young married couple, Laura and Julio, and an enigmatic neighbor named Manuel, who lives in the apartment next door. Manuel is a bohemian type who refers to himself as a writer, although he is still to write anything. Over the course of 2 years, he becomes a fixture in the married couple's apartment. His magnetic personality begins to be an essential facet of Laura and Julio's life together.

And then, boom, he is involved in a serious accident and left clinging to life in a coma. The authorities find a note saying they should contact Laura and Julio in case of emergency. This having been done, they soon realize, in spite of the close relationship that's been forged, they know virtually nothing about Manuel. They have no clues as to next of kin or who to contact until Julio remembers Manuel once said his father was a diplomat. He informs the Foreign Ministry. Two days later he is waiting for the father to arrive at the hospital.

And this is where the aforementioned resonant phrases appeared.

Obviously, Julio had no idea as to what Manuel's father would look like, but he recognized him from a "100 meters away," not because of their discernible physical likeness, but from the way he carried himself and interacted with the world around him. There was a "distinction" here that had nothing to do with the elegance of the clothes he wore, a wardrobe his son had no vocation for. And yet, it was just this shared "distinction" that made the father immediately recognizable for Julio. Millas, through the thoughts of Julio, puts it like this:

"La distincion venia de adentro." Being distinguished came from within.

The interlude in the hospital goes on for another page or two. This seemingly innate distinguished quality the father-diplomat exudes so effortlessly, becomes the focus of Julio's experience that day. I quote some excerpts of Julio's thoughts as set forth in the novel. "People like Manuel and his father (...) they dressed from the inside out. Upon rising in the morning, they first got their emotional side in place, and over this emotional being came the inner organs, and over the inner organs came the muscles, until the final layer, the clothes, came to rest. He, on the other hand, dressed from the outside in, (...) hoping that exterior layer of decoration would conjure up an original character, a unique thought, perhaps an unusual way of confronting the world."

Whereas Julio dressed in order to try and be distinctive, the clothes of Manuel and his father were little more than the outer appendages of their natural distinction. Julio tried to make his clothes the vehicle of who he hoped to be; the clothes of Manuel and his father were the result of who they were.

One would be challenged to find a person who did not want to be considered a "distinguished" person, which is just another way to say who others respect and respond to as such a person would want. Millas' penetration into the soul (remember, it comes from within) of such a person, is illuminating. It explains something we might already have some understanding of, but cannot express clearly to ourselves. He provides the key to open that door.

But I quarrel with the stingy nature of the great writer's depiction of this distinguished quality. He seems to suggest, perhaps unconsciously, that the demographic of this quality trait is the almost exclusive province of our upper classes. Manuel's father is a diplomat, they obviously come from a financially well-accommodated lineage, and Millas presents their distinction as a harmonious result of this. It leaves the impression that distinction is mainly a product of this small group.

Being a "distinguished" person crosses all the barriers we humans have erected in delineating ourselves. Although it might take on different exterior ways of manifesting itself, it could appear at any time amongst any constituency. We might not like to admit it, but we all carry around some residual baggage sprung from an upbringing that defined who <u>you</u> are and who <u>they</u> are. There is a little bit of snob in all of us, meant to stroke our concepts of self worth. We usually enter into contact with others with these almost subconscious prejudices intact. They generally won't be broken down until we begin to know the inner worth of a person, a process that takes some degree of personal contact.

That anonymous garbage man you see passing by every third day or so, in his less than elegant, grease stained work clothes, could very well be a "distinguished" person.

Hopefully, the reader will forgive the following self indulgence as I tell the story I promised near the beginning of this essay, for its relevance in the never ending quest for truth and enlightenment this mass of dubious philosophical patter strives for, is considered reason enough for inclusion, all fears of crass self indulgence aside.

Not too long ago, a relative of mine visited the town where I live. Upon arrival at the airport, she was forced to use the services of the company I work for. Knowing of such employment, she asked the person she was dealing with if he knew me. I shall call this person Louis, and he is not without his own interesting life story, being a son of the deep south whose lyrical accent and love of football are the only 2 vestiges left from the youth of a man who has transcended a very provincial origin (how‘s that for some subtle prejudice?). As is logical, Louis said he knew me and a brief dissertation ensued.

Later that day, my relative paraphrased what Louis had told her. He said I was not the kind of person one talked to just to talk – how ya' doin', nice weather, and other such forms of mundane chit chat – and that he never said anything to me unless he really had something to say, something that mattered.

I have little money, don't know how to "dress," nor do I come from a social class with inherent qualities of distinction, but what Louis said about me has a rather "distinguished" quality ... don't you think?

Relevant Material: A rich landowner running for political office in Spain's first elections after Franco's dictatorship, offers one of his poor agricultural workers 25 *pesetas* if he will vote for him. The "peon" throws the coins at the owner's feet and exclaims, "*con mi propia hambre, mando yo!*" With my own hunger, I rule! From the novel, "La Senda del Drago" (The Path of the Drago), by the Spaniard, Jorge Sampedro.

THE DATE PALM

(6/09, Spain)

In the essay "Doctors, II" I spoke of a date palm I've known since it was a child. Its story continues in this essay, but in order to understand the complete biography, the following historical data is necessary:

This particular date palm finds its home on the grounds of the exquisite little hotel by the Roman Sea I've been frequenting for more than 20 years. The hotel itself is an elongated, 2 story structure, about 80 yards in length, oriented, more or less, along a southeast-northwest axis. About 15 years ago, they built a small addition onto the north side of the building. Not having any more property to the north, the owners added an L-shaped wing to the original structure, thus creating a horseshoe like enclosure on this side of the hotel. A small garden that had always existed on this side, now found itself enclosed in the horseshoe.

About 10 years ago, in this small garden situated in the horseshoe, someone decided to plant a date palm – probably Paquita or Katina, sisters who are third generation owners of the hotel, who have made it into the delightful place it is today. All living things born to this planet, be they plant, animal or whatever, find themselves in the environment they will have to deal with, with the conditions that dictate the quality of their lives. Amongst certain higher species of the animal world, some ability to make the best or worst of the environment dealt them in the poker game of life, may be evident, but even amongst the clods we call human beings, who seem to have the most ability to overcome these roulette wheel whims of fate, the hand they are dealt is usually very indicative of what they get out of life.

On a scale of 1 to 10, 1 being I never should have been born here and won't survive my infancy, and 10 being this is the ideal place for me, one where the fullest expression of my species can be attained, the date palm in the horseshoe enclosure gets a 9.9. In less than a decade, its top leaves are reaching 25 feet above the ground, an accomplishment that pales in comparison to the impenetrable thickness of its cross-thatched bark, and a circumference at its base that 2 human beings could not encircle in their outstretched arms. Such girth suggests a powerful root system below, one that firmly anchors the perfect straight up posture of a magnificent example of this dry weather, desert palm, one that gives forth with a regular bounty of its most sublime achievement, its crop of thick, juicy dates.

This is Maria Muldaur's midnight at the oasis, put those camels to bed.

There is really only one species that could now put this wonderful tree into a survival crisis, and I think we all know which one that is. If you need a little help, it's the only one that includes, unfortunately for all species, Glenn Beck. Certainly, given the historical evidence of this species, the possibility of one of its innumerable bellicose confrontations and the horrifying destruction these actions are capable of, is never an unthinkable concept, albeit a remote one in this part of the world's left field. A more pressing concern is the destruction inherent in this species' commercial activity. For some members of this species, a glittering new condo would make them happier (or so they think) than some get-in-the-way date palm, sitting there making nobody any money. Given the mindset of the people currently in charge of the date palm, as well as the prevailing attitude of the island where it exists, this is only a remote possibility, even in the long run. As a result, in assessing the totality of the environmental data concerning this date palm, both physically and emotionally, it could be looking at a longevity figure somewhat akin to immortality.

In the words of Smokey Robinson, "I'll second that emotion."

If we ponder the environmental evidence, the spectacular triumph of this tree seems explicable. Foremost here could be the horseshoe structure that surrounds it on 3 sides and the directional orientation of such. The most vicious blows of nature in these parts, both in frigidity and force, come from the northern blasts of the planet's less temperate zones. The less of this the tree might have to bear, the happier it would be. With the hotel's horseshoe on the northern side of the building, the tree's most vulnerable flanks are strongly fortified. Nice and cozy. If the L-shaped extension had been put on the south side of the building, thus leaving the northern side of the horseshoe open, chances are, a nice little garden with a huge date palm as its main protagonist, would be a more mottled, stunted affair, with a botanical result far less attractive.

All other factors are well within the positive, especially sunlight, which is always a desert species' bread and butter. Its enclosure in the horseshoe might have retarded access to this element, but, like a child born into a well to do family, the wheel of fortune has spun its way once again. The open side of the horseshoe, due to the sun's daily path and its relationship to the exact orientation of the building, receives blinding amounts of sun.

Within the next year or so, a change in the great date palm's life is about to happen, one that should make it even happier. Its height is about to clear the limit of the building that surrounds it on 3 sides. It will emerge into a much larger world, one far more in contact with all the elements around it. It will begin to experience a greater range of sensations from an environment it hadn't had full access to. At one time, this may have endangered its survival or retarded its growth, but the firm foundation created in its most formative years has erased such concerns. It has dug a deep toehold into its own survival, such that it now seems inexpugnable. It is time to come out. Bring it on. Wind, rain, sun, cold – life in its full expression. Without being a scientific expert of any kind, I'd guess the big date palm is going to love it.

Now that we've come this far, it's time to tell the reader that the date palm referred to in this essay's title is not the big beauty we've been talking about up until now. All that was just background, table setting, perhaps a bit more than necessary for the telling of this tale, but hey! who's in charge here? When it comes to art, poetry and blah-blah-blah, there are no frontiers. This is all within the natural scheme of things, be it for date palms or unknown essayists, the combinations are something like infinite, and the seeds will fall, prosper or shrivel where they may.

Anyhoo – as already mentioned in such essays as "Music," "O.J." and "The Cell Phone," the hotel which is the setting for this tale is situated on a beautiful body of water the locals refer to as "El Lago" (the lake). This is a misnomer, for although it looks like a lake, it is really an arm of the Mediterranean that enters through a small opening in an otherwise impenetrable spit of land that separates it from the open sea. The inner side of the hotel fronts El Lago and is buffered from it by a ten-yard strip of sandy beach. A beautiful "*terrazza,*" imbued with the usual refreshments and gastronomic possibilities demanded by that hedonistic creature known as the "tourist," overlooks the splendor of it all.

The first thing I noticed upon arrival this year, was a diminutive baby date palm struggling for life – all by its lonesome, in the open – right in the middle of the beach in question. Like babies of all species, it was cute, an adorable, one-foot high version of the colossus its species has the potential to be. The few leaves it had already unfurled were unmistakable miniature replicas of the real thing, but best of all was about 3 inches worth of bark that had formed at its base. It was young, tender and weak, but it was already a lovely facsimile of an adult, like an authentic model train.

I sat down on the terrazza and began reading a book, but the little date palm kept calling my attention. Like Darwin in the Galapagos, I studied the survival possibilities of the little tusker, all alone and at risk on the naked beach. I felt empathy for it, maybe even something bordering on affection. I closed my book and stepped down onto the beach to get a closer look. Some wind had damaged one of the lower palm leaves and its green color was beginning to fade, giving the toddler a scruffy look. But lower leaves are supposed to fall off date palms and there was nothing to suggest a health problem. I gently closed my hand around the 3 inches of bark that had developed at its base. Although I could easily yank it out of the ground, I could feel its tenuous root system beginning to grab a firm hold on the planet. It had claimed this homestead for itself and was making its stand.

How nice it would be if the baby sprout made it, and the beach could profit from its shade and beauty. What a good idea, I thought, to plant it there.

About a half hour later, now back on the terrazza and more immersed in my book, the 4th generation in the person of my good friend Pau (see essay "Who Owns Your Brain?"), strolled onto the terrazza. I asked, "Pau, who planted the little date palm on the beach?" He looked at me like it was a dumb question, and I immediately knew my mistake. It was the natural offspring of the big tree in the horseshoe. The dates grow, they fall off the tree, they dry up, they get blown about in the pinball machine of the elements, and voila! – on occasion, the earth gets impregnated.

Pau motioned me over to the edge of the terrazza and pointed down the beach. About 30 yards away was a little palm tree, now about 3 feet high, pinned against the wall of the terrazza and somewhat more anonymous amidst some bushes and weeds. In addition, there were 4 babies right under the big tree in the horseshoe garden, youngsters I'd already noticed the year before. Their proximity to mom made their origins obvious, even to a city slicker like me.

Of all the siblings in this new generation, the baby on the beach was undoubtedly the most charismatic. Its gamble with life was the riskiest bet of all, but, ironically, its chance for fame and glory was the greatest. Its siblings were far more secure in their ability to survive, having been born in more logical places for their genesis, but their long-range possibilities were limited.

If we return to a Darwinian mindset and examine the environmental facts, it made sense for the palm against the terrazza wall to be born there. The on shore wind had piled some dirt up against it that the off shore wind would not return in kind. The same could be said for any vegetable seeds blown against the wall. That is where they'd stay and where some of them would eventually sprout. A light beard of grass had grown there, along with some other more unruly proletarian forms of plant life, solidifying the ground a bit, holding a bit more water – and there you are: with the big date palm in the horseshoe providing the fecundity, another date palm, now big enough to be called a small child, was growing along the terrazza wall. The small vegetable province that had taken hold there would keep those bumbling-stumbling humans at bay, the wall offered some protection from the elements, how good it is to be alive, but –

If we return to the Galapagos and further delve into the survival of the species, the date palm by the terrazza wall has almost no possibilities to excel. The wall itself severely limits its sphere of operations, but even more telling is an impending conflict with those bleepity-bleep humans. The terrazza wall is the frontier of a fine restaurant overlooking the spectacular view of El Lago, its environs, and a larger island to the north. No act of nature would be allowed to impede this view, nor would any encroachment from its growth be tolerated on the terrazza. Chances are, this date palm, secure in its youth, will never get the chance to express itself further.

Much the same is true for the kids now enjoying themselves by the side of their magnificent mother. It is a safe and secure crib for the moment, but trying to make a name for oneself in the shadow of the giant would seem close to impossible. Perhaps in the wild, out there at Maria Muldaur's midnight oasis, they'd be part of those thick stands of date palms – like mini-jungles of date palms – I'd seen while traveling across North Africa. But here in the horseshoe garden there is no room for that. Their only chance for excellence is to be transplanted – someone wants to plant a date palm, etc. – not an impossible occurrence according to Pau.

That leaves the little fella' on the beach, the date palm for whom this essay was named, the one with the star quality, the one with "it." Yes, it is in harm's way out there, with those pesky humans frolicking about. At this stage of its life, a wayward soccer ball could close the books on it, or some kids chasing each other, or a blown over beach umbrella – adios. And who knows what havoc the elements could assault it with at its totally undefended position. But it has already made it through one winter and is still in the game. Just a few more feet of growth; another few inches of bark; a deeper toehold in the earth, and its long-range prognosis would improve notably. It's doubtful it could ever be the gorgeous diva its mother is. The battering it will have to endure from its exposed location and the more impoverished quality of its sandy beach soil, will conspire in limiting its size and beauty, but it has all the room in the world to expand in, free of competition. It has a monopoly on any resources it is privy to. If we paraphrase the words of that great boxer-longshoremen, Marlon Brando, "I could be somebody."

Only time will tell.

Thank you for reading.
Please review this book. Reviews help others find me and inspires me to keep writing!

If you would like to be put on our email list to receive updates on new releases, contests, and promotions, please go to AbsolutelyAmazingEbooks.com and sign up.

ACKNOWLEDGMENTS

For one who has wandered almost 40 years in the wilderness of literary anonymity, those who showed interest in my work long before the appearance of this book have a special place in my heart. Without there being any particular order in importance, such people as the musician, Michael Dann, the writers Mike Mewshaw and his son Marc, Kathy Hoisington (may she rest in peace), the economist-commentator Rick Boettger, my sister and her husband, Linda and Leonard Lipson, she of the superior intellect, Sally Reno, the Renaissance couple, Joel and Erica Biddle, the writer Rick Skwiot, "uncle" Bill the dispatcher, as well as others, gave me the confidence to keep "doing my thing".

Worthy of special mention is the writer John Leslie, who pointed me in the right direction without me even having to ask him.

ABOUT THE AUTHOR

Jerome Grapel was born in Brooklyn, NY in 1945 and raised in the New York City area in what could be called a vintage middle class upbringing. He attended Temple University in Philadelphia where he played baseball and graduated with a B.A. in history in 1967. With a noticeable lack of vocation for anything, and not knowing what else to do, he continued at Temple Law School, graduating in 1970.

After a short stint at a small law firm, Grapel's courtship with the American Dream ended unsuccessfully. In 1972, a friend from college introduced him to Key West, the perfect antidote for cultural misfits. He has lived there ever since, working a multitude of inconsequential jobs, none of which had to be taken home with him. For the last 30 years he has been driving a taxi, a job which offered the flexibility to travel extensively. Without a "career" to encumber much of his life, he began writing in his spare time. "I found out this is what I want to do," he says.

Grapel has been married 2 times but has grown accustomed to living alone over the last 20 years or so. It is also relevant to note that for much of that time he has spent 2 months of the year on the Spanish island of Formentera.

The New Atlantian Library

NewAtlantianLibrary.com
or AbsolutelyAmazingEbooks.com
or AA-eBooks.com

www.ingramcontent.com/pod-product-compliance
Lightning Source LLC
Chambersburg PA
CBHW061002280326
41935CB00009B/802

* 9 7 8 0 6 1 5 9 9 6 3 5 6 *